What people are saying about Simple Community:

"Simple Community delivers a seriously needed message at just the right time. The Living side of the book helps us all understand how we lost community and the Building side shows us how to get it back. In this very short book you are sure to find a handful of new insights that will simply add more joy and value to the time you spend with your family, friends, and neighbors. And if it really grabs you, "Simple Community" will show you ways to do far more for your community than you thought possible before you picked up the book."

Ken Dychtwald, Ph.D., best-selling author of *With Purpose: Going from Success to Significance in Work and Life*

....

"I found Simple Community to be insightful, compelling in its approach and an absolute joy to read. I found myself nodding my head in agreement on many occasions. It outlines a vision for the personal and economic development of our future and points us in a positive direction. If asked what I thought of it I would likely reply — If you are ready for some serious thinking about the future of America, then I suggest you read this book."

Robert Kanaby, Executive Director of the National Federation of State High School Associations (NFHS)

....

"Stories are the proof that life has taken place when people gather. That thought alone from Simple Community makes this book worth reading. Most of the books I write are really story books about the best things that happen between people. Rich has taken the importance of stories to another level. After reading Simple Community you will recognize the power of your life stories to encourage those around you and motivate more of the best of simple community."

Ronda Rich, best-selling author of *What Southern Women Know About Faith*

....

"Simple Community is both easy and challenging to read—easy because so much of it rings true and is written in a personal style; challenging because the insights offered are sobering. Suggestions are practical, realistic and attainable. Rich's book shows that it takes only a little time and effort to benefit by extending community— the payoff quickly outweighs the efforts involved."

Mike Racy, Vice President of Division II, The National Collegiate Athletic Association

"If you are in business, Simple Community will be like LASIK surgery enabling you to more clearly see who to reach and what to do once you are there with them. In essence, Simple Community has defined the intersection between life and consumer marketing. For years, brands have tried to find tangible ways to invest in community and build business. Rich has provided the road map to do just that."

Tim Schoen, Vice President, Sports & Entertainment Marketing, Anheuser-Busch/InBev

....

"Minor League Baseball is all about community. Understanding the role that our clubs play within there respective communities is the cornerstone of any successful club. "Simple Community" provides great insight into why Minor League Baseball has been such an integral part of these locales and goes beyond that to show us how to find the best of community when we are away from the local ball park too."

John Cook, Senior Vice President, Business Operations, Minor League Baseball

....

"Luker makes two seemingly unconnected observations: society is increasingly in need of opportunities for Simple Community. Advertisers are experiencing declining returns from their information campaigns. However Luker makes a strong case that the business sector can help society in its quest for more community and reap the benefits for their product at the same time. Luker's 25 years in research, coupled with a deep sense of the human condition, gives him a vantage point to call for a paradigm shift in advertising. This book is a must read for citizens and advertisers alike."

Jerome Johnston, Ph.D., Research Professor, University of Michigan and author of *Positive Images: Breaking Stereotypes with Children's Television*

....

"Rich has found a way to enrich the relationship between college and college town at a time when both are finding it harder to make ends meet. His book – and his work – are unusually sensitive to the differing needs of various groups who work and live together in community. Rich's years working with NCAA Division II schools have paid off in Simple Community which is a guide that makes it easier for schools and organizations of all kinds to work together. The approach will lead to more fulfilling community, better education, and more cooperation among us all."

Dr. Charles Ambrose, President, Pfeiffer University and Immediate Past Chair, NCAA Division II Presidents Council -

Richard Luker, Ph.D.

With the publication of Simple Community, Rich is now turning his attention to helping communities, organizations and American companies work together to enrich community life in America. Rich's background leading to Simple Community is covered in the preface to the book. Rich and his wife Vicki live in Fairview, NC and St. Petersburg, FL.

Building Simple Community

By
Rich Luker, Ph.D.

Published by Tangeness Press, St. Petersburg, FL
Printed in the United States of America
Library of Congress Control Number: 2009929066
"Simple community" (ISBN 9780615299112)

Acknowledgements

I have an entire community to thank for their thoughts and contributions to this book. Topping the list is Caitlin Bonham who has read it and commented on it at least as many times as I have. If you enjoy the read, you have Caitlin to thank for that.

David Pickle, the managing director of publishing for the NCAA is responsible for introducing my community work to the NCAA in the first place. Beyond that, he kindly took the time to suggest the structure for the book which I ultimately adopted. David introduced me to Arnel Reynon who designed the cover and produced the layout and art for the book. Thanks Arnel.

Several people read various versions and provided helpful advice along the way. Chandra Lim and Sara Whitaker in particular challenged me on several key concepts in the book. Other helpful readers included Dennis Boyle, Leo Fitzpatrick, Alison Jenks, Abby Bennett, and Judy Shoemaker.

I am deeply indebted to the NCAA and NFHS for the opportunity to work with them on creating community engagement strategies. I can't possibly name everyone involved but I need to single out a few in each organization who share my passion for building community and worked tirelessly to make it happen in their organizations.

In the NCAA that would include Division II Vice President Mike Racy, and Director, Terri Steeb. During the development of the strategy Dr. Chuck Ambrose, was the Chairman of the Division II Presidents and Chancellors Council. He served two terms. Chuck was the ideal leader for this strategy. At the same time,

Jill Willson was the head of the Division II Management Council. If there was anyone more supportive (still) of the community initiative than Jill, I don't know who it is. I consider them all friends. I also owe a big debt of gratitude to the members of the committee who worked with me to develop the overall strategy. Dennis Cryder and JoJo Rinebold are long time friends and were steadfast supporters throughout the development of the strategy.

Judy Shoemaker, the head of Marketing for NFHS, has been the champion of community within NFHS. She brought me in to speak to the group initially and has worked side-by-side with me ever since. With her love and commitment to the development of high school students combined with a stellar marketing career, she was the ideal person to assure a high school community strategy would remain honest to the mission of NFHS and provide for needs into the future. That said, the incredible passion for the well-being of students, and the friendship and support of NFHS executive director Robert Kanaby and Robert Gardner, the chief operating officer are both deeply appreciated. Finally, I am honored with the trust of the NFHS Board of Directors and state executives in the support they have shown for the community strategy.

I also want to mention two people I met by chance on separate occasions while flying across America. First, Pat O'Connor had just become President of Minor League Baseball when we met. Thanks to Pat (and John Cook), I have been able to more actively support community initiatives with MiLB.

My second chance encounter was with Susan S. who is a member of a family who owns a noted American company. I was working on the book on the flight and she asked me about it. Her kind words and encouragement went a long way toward developing new, more community-friendly ways of opening doors at major American companies.

I sought advice from many people about how best to distribute the book once it was finished. In particular, I want to thank Ken Dychtwald, who has published more than a dozen books on aging, for his help throughout. Doris Michaels took time from her agency to provide helpful advice on the publishing process as well. My friends C. J. Lonoff, Jan Fermback and Stephanie Reaves were among the earliest to support the idea of writing in the first place and to encourage me when I was having a hard time getting started.

Finally, to my Myrtle Beach buddies, Duane, Lou and Dan, many thanks for being my Simple Community for more than thirty years.

Dedication

This book is dedicated to my wife
and true partner in everything I do,
Vicki, and our children
(Anna, Melissa, Dan and Abby).

Table of Contents

Read this side of the book first if...

- You are looking for a better alternative to more advertising
- You are a brand executive looking to form real relationships
- You believe in the value of community and are ready to build it
- You are looking for a realistic way to bring scale to grassroots marketing
- You work at a school and want the support of your community
- You are trying to find a way to support community gathering

Preface

For years I have been speaking to groups about the importance of people gathering with their friends and family. For nearly as long, the audiences have been encouraging me to write a book on the subject.

By studying history and through my own research I have become very passionate about the importance, the need for and the lack of community, Simple Community – playful, enjoyable time with others, without an agenda or work objective. It seems the passion is contagious. The more time passes, the more often I get asked to speak to groups about Simple Community. I wish I could always say yes, but I can't anymore. Besides, I don't think that my presentations alone will do enough to encourage people to live their lives with more Simple Community. This book is my attempt to reach farther with a message that will hopefully encourage people to make the enjoyment of time with others a higher priority in their lives.

I have been studying everyday American life for over 25 years. It started with a growing concern that American teens were struggling with life's purpose and with developing quality relationships. For my doctoral dissertation in graduate school I studied theories of adolescent social development and conducted a series of studies with American teens on the quality of their relationships with parents, individual friends and peer groups. I wondered if American teens turned to TV and other media when they felt distressed. I am happy to say, the research found that the vast majority of American teens have strong nurturing relationships, which provide them with the support they need. The minority of American adolescents who do struggle rarely rely on the media as a source of support or direction.

Despite the overall good news, my research left one enduring question going back to the first study in 1979. We know that relationships produce many benefits including increased health and happiness. So why isn't enjoyment of others a higher priority in American culture today? There are dozens of books about how communities can and should "work" together. They focus on community service – working for the good of others – or community activism – fighting for the rights of others. They advocate empowering communities – how to influence government and commerce to provide needed resources. All are important, serious needs. But I could not find one book on why or how we should play together as neighbors and communities for the good of all. Play for the good of all – it even sounds frivolous.

I arrived at an understanding of the need for Simple Community by a curious path. It took nearly twenty years to fully grasp it.

For most of my career I have studied the concept of free time and how Americans spend their time when they don't have to work, go to school, or fulfill other obligations. The most telling finding from that research is that most Americans believe they have substantially less free time than they actually do. If you ask people how much free time they have, they usually say little to none. But when you work with them to figure out how they have spent their time recently, they usually discover that they have far more than they realized.

"I am too busy to get together with you." Perception is reality. If we think we have less time, we live that way. We minimize or reduce the amount of time we choose to spend enjoying each other's company. Even though I repeatedly saw in the studies that we feel we have little time, I didn't connect it with our need to prioritize enjoying time with others. I am certainly far more guilty than most of doing serious things at the expense of the truly fulfilling and valuable enjoyment of others. But I didn't realize it until I understood the need for Simple Community.

In the early part of my career, while I taught at Temple University, I studied the role of television in American society and consulted on the creation of television shows that sought to provide a blend of entertainment and educational content. A bad year for baseball on television started me on the path of researching the role of sports that led to my study of community.

When CBS lost hundreds of millions of dollars in one year on their investment to broadcast Major League Baseball (MLB) games, I asked a team of graduate students to find the research that CBS or MLB used to arrive at the financial value of rights to broadcast those games. They found nothing. In 1988 there was not one significant study dedicated to the role of sports in American life. Not one, even though the sports industry generated billions in revenue every year.

In response, I spent years studying sports in general and then approached ESPN in 1993 with a business plan to systematically study sports in America. My work culminated in the creation of the ESPN Sports Poll which was launched in January of 1994. In over 15 years of nearly daily interviewing, over 200,000 Americans have been surveyed on their broad interests and sports activities. Over that time, more than 2,000 different questions have been included to monitor the overall landscape of sports in America. Through the ESPN Sports Poll I was able to watch the National Football League overtake Major League Baseball as America's favorite sport in 1994 – the year the MLB season ended early because of a strike.

But the Sports Poll became an important measure of the role of sports in America as we studied the connection between sports and how Americans handled hard times. Following 9/11 I was able to provide insight to the sports leagues, media and sponsors on how Americans felt about sports during a crisis. Many sponsors were considering withdrawing from sports sponsorship altogether until it was over. There were discussions of canceling the remainder of sports seasons. But the research told us that we needed the exact opposite. During the worst of times we need relief. During bad times we are comforted by spending and enjoying time with those we love. We know this from the research during the decline of tech stocks at the end of the 1990s and again in a major economic crisis in 2008. During hard times, Americans need relief and they see time with friends and family and the enjoyment of sports as a key source of relief.

It took more to fully understand the need for Simple Community than the realization that sports and other sources of fun provide relief. While I was studying the history of how free time activity and interest in sports in America changed over time since the 1800s, I came to the realization that how we work together, not specifically what we do, seems to be the strongest connection to what we like and turn to as a source of relief. A major section of Simple Community is devoted to America's transition from agriculture to manufacturing to service as the primary source of how we make a living. The service economy no longer provides the time, place and natural contexts for gathering that were common to farming and manufacturing economies.

One final, key piece of the need for Simple Community became clear to me as Internet use took hold in America. Many people seem to think "social networking" through digital media will provide all the community we need. I disagree. Being in the same place at the same time is at the heart of relationships. New technologies provide us with more enhanced ways to communicate when we can't be together, but mediated communication will never replace being there.

Being a technology-driven, service-based economy makes it easier for us to work alone and readily change what we do for a living from time to time. Work is no longer a way of life, it is just a job. I am convinced that our realization that Simple Community, playfulness, and recreation are necessities, not optional niceties, is way overdue. They provide relief in distressing times. Simple Community re-creates us. It allows us to replenish our energy, recharge the batteries, and remind ourselves that we work as hard as we do for the sake of being in a community with those we love.

With the need more clearly understood, the major breakthrough for developing Simple Community came in 2005 when I was asked by the National Collegiate Athletic Association (NCAA) to address the first large meeting of Division II college presidents and chancellors on the topic of building community on college campuses. I had first talked about colleges as town squares in 2004 because it seemed to me that colleges were the last remaining, financially supported context able to provide Simple Community to a significant group of people. Shortly after my presentation to the NCAA Division II presidents they committed to developing a significant strategy to encourage broader community activity on their campuses and they asked me to lead the effort. I worked on the creation and activation of that strategy with an advisory group comprised of people in key positions in Division II schools for the next 18 months. The key goal was to enable greater connection between students, the campus community and the larger neighborhood of those who live near the school.

Early on we realized that our best resource to enable schools to work together would be the creation of a website to provide tips on how to reach out to the community. An important element of the website was a section providing ideas that worked on individual campuses. Our belief was schools would be most motivated and encouraged by following the successes of other schools. The website was launched in February, 2007. It was intended for the internal use of the roughly 300 schools of Division II and was not publicized outside the regularly distributed information to those schools. I think everyone would have been thrilled if, by the end of 2008, we had 25,000 visitors to the website from people trying to build Simple Community. As I write this preface in January, 2009, there have been over 350,000 visits to the site. Simple Community has taken root in ways we could not have predicted and I am convinced that we are just seeing the beginning of the success and positive impact that Division II schools – and other colleges and universities will experience – as they actively open their doors to the community.

At the beginning of 2008 I started working with the National Federation of State High School Associations (NFHS) on a parallel strategy for high schools titled "Facilitating Community," which was adopted by the Board of Directors in

2009. If college campuses are the town squares, high schools are the neighborhood centers. The work with NFHS has been well received and will produce tremendous opportunities for high schools around America to offer richer experiences for their students. At the same time, the strategy is creating new opportunities for adults in the community who do not have students at the school to become more involved through the broad range of activities offered by the high school.

I did not start my career thinking I would devote my life to building Simple Community. It just turned out that way. From the time I completed my doctoral work I have engaged in academic/scholarly work, maintaining faculty status pretty much throughout the years, currently at Northwestern University. At the same time, I have always believed it is important and valuable to find ways to utilize scholarly learning to improve the quality of life, so I have worked in the commercial sector for most of my post-graduate years. The combination of those experiences is vital to this book. My scholarly work has given me perspective on American social life. My commercial work has allowed me to see the opportunity for the American business community to do more to enable Simple Community in a way that also helps their business. If given the choice between exposure to 1,000 advertisements, or one community experience made possible by a relevant company, which would you choose? Just now, American companies are beginning to realize that there is much to be gained by investing in the real lives of people. Consider, for example, the proliferation of corporate "green" initiatives and advertising campaigns which show sensitivity to the need to protect the environment.

Simple Community is my attempt to tie together 25 years of work and research on the importance of – the need for – greater opportunities for us to gather and enjoy each other. I continue to be surprised that we don't realize this on our own, but, for whatever reason, many, if not most of us, feel guilty about investing in the enjoyment of life. We do not recognize it for the necessity it is. By reading and passing along the thoughts in this book I hope you will be able to embrace, build and find more Simple Community in your life and with those you love.

I have presented most of what you are about to read to audiences dozens of times. At this point, it is almost impossible for me to think about this material as a writer rather than as a speaker. This book is not intended to be a piece of literature. Please read it for the message.

(The preface is the same for Living Simple Community.)

CHAPTER 1
Good Reasons to Read Building Simple Community

The vast majority of us do not live in isolation. Being around people, however, is not the same thing as spending meaningful time with them. American families and friends used to have more face-to-face time than we do today. The other side of this book is all about how we lost that time and about the things we all can do to restore a greater sense of belonging. I call it Simple because our desire is not for something complex and certainly not for something we have to work hard at to achieve. Just as grassroots movements are formed by everyday people who desire change, Simple Community starts with individuals who do small things to bring people together. Companies and organizations in America can do a lot to help those people. I wrote Building Simple Community to encourage that investment.

More often than not, when I talk to marketing executives about investing in community the conversation begins in an atmosphere of clear skepticism. More often than not, it ends with two conclusions. Building community with scale is possible, and it is the right thing to do.

Companies are already investing in the environment because it is the right thing to do. The value of investing in community can be two-fold – It will enable more people to spend fulfilling time with family and friends. And, at the same time, will allow businesses to reestablish meaningful relationships with customers, like back in the day when Bob ran the local hardware store.

Many, if not most, major American companies would invest considerably more in grassroots marketing if they could realize "scale" – the ability to support hundreds, even thousands, of activities without having to manage them individually. It is possible. We can realize scale in grassroots programs by enabling three groups of people to work together with the ideas in this book. Those people are: Individuals who enjoy bringing families, friends and neighbors together; marketing professionals who want to invest in grassroots marketing; and people who manage places where people naturally gather (schools, parks, and others). Building Simple Community provides a foundation for those three groups to work together more meaningfully.

MARKETING PROFESSIONALS
Here are four ways the concepts in this book can help you:

1. Make your grassroots marketing efforts more appreciated: Your grassroots programs can be more meaningfully involved with and contribute to your customers' lives with a new approach that takes the current and pressing needs of people into sharper consideration. The result is providing resources to communities without blatantly selling. In fact, brands are encouraged to invest only when and where their products and services are relevant and can enhance people's lives. When a brand fits the community needs of its consumers, the people who use those resources will appreciate and remember them the next time they buy.

2. Realize the potential for attainable, scalable grassroots. Contributing to one neighborhood picnic won't get you much recognition or consumer loyalty. However, if you could easily replicate a meaningful experience at hundreds or thousands of picnics, you would be well on your way to success. Brands and the organizations able to host people and experiences need a unified approach. By understanding and sharing the ideas that follow, and adding to the foundation that is already being built by the organizations that have hundreds or thousands of places to gather at the local level, scalable grassroots can be a reality.

3. Powerfully integrate grassroots activities with emerging new media marketing. Your products and services have qualities that can naturally enhance people's quality of life when they are together face-to-face. Grassroots activities can accent the heart of your brand. New media tools like blogs, websites, and social networking will allows people to continue these experiences day-to-day by providing information, calendars and locations of

daily opportunities for community gathering. You will find that stories are a key component to Simple Community. In the work I have already done we have learned that the ability to share stories through the electronic media goes a long way toward extending participation.

4. Respond and invest appropriately during times in which corporate investments have come under extreme scrutiny. In the fall of 2008, America was entering the worst economic period since the Great Depression. Companies were decreasing or discontinuing sponsorship of sports and other entertainment and canceling meetings and conferences for fear they would be seen as inappropriate or insensitive. At the same time, many companies were looking for ways to contribute to constructive efforts and turned to environmental sensitivity (green) initiatives and social responsibility programs. Research from previous American recessions and from the weeks following September 11th, 2001, clearly showed that Americans wanted and appreciated the relief that community affords and that they wanted companies to continue supporting those activities. Research in December, 2008 confirmed those findings.

ORGANIZATIONAL LEADERS

National, regional, and local leaders of schools, parks, places of worship and other locations that are suitable for gathering will find at least four good reasons to keep reading. Building Simple Community will help you find ways to:

1. Enable more fulfilled community involvement. The actual places where enjoyable social gathering can occur are considerably less accessible than most people realize. If your organization has access to areas like theaters, halls, or gymnasiums, you can find ways to create new opportunities for your members or do more with the activities that you already provide.

2. Share community-gathering ideas that will increase the value of your organization to your neighborhood. Many individual member locations of organizations have come up with successful ideas to be a more active part of their neighborhoods in ways that others in the organization have not yet thought of. Building Simple Community has suggestions for how you can identify and share those successes with others.

3. Gain support in your local community by offering them more

opportunities for enjoyable gathering. If your organization is already involved in community service, you are doing important work to improve the living conditions of your neighbors. Simple Community meets a different need. If your location is conducive for enjoyable social gathering, Building Simple Community will show you how you can help to provide the low-intensity social relief that all Americans need.

4. Get significant resource support and investment from companies and organizations. The best ideas can be extended even further when companies and other organizations supply resources that naturally fit the purpose of your activity. Building Simple Community will show you how to find and work with those resources.

CHAPTER 2
Simple Community

I have researched American social life for over 25 years. The findings of the vast majority of those studies indicate that people identify spending more time with family and friends as what they need – and lack – the most. How can we be around people all the time and still have this need? Life in America has changed. Specifically, how we work has changed. The consequence of those changes, which took place over the past two centuries, is that we have lost a significant amount of the opportunities to spend time with the people we care about.

Farmers, manufacturers and service workers

For much of the 1800s America was a farming culture. Over half of everything we produced was agricultural. Families worked on farms and had to spend most of their waking hours together to pay the bills. Personal bonds arose naturally from their way of life and they could enjoy each other's company while they worked. The most popular sports in the early and mid 1800s were boxing, barn wrestling and horse racing – all sports associated with and easily conducted on farms. The aspects of life that are now separated into work and leisure were still blended together. At the height of the agricultural age, the economy was driven by families working together on farms and family was at the heart of American culture.

By the mid 1900s the dominant source of work in America had shifted from farming to manufacturing. People came together in towns to work in factories, mines and office buildings. They had cars and other forms of transportation that allowed them to gather daily for work. People moved to be closer to their place of work and the new communities got together after work and on weekends. The heart of American culture migrated from family to community. The most popular sport in the mid 1900s was baseball, a community-based sport. Teams were identified and supported by their towns and cities. Work continued to dictate how and where we lived. Similar to the agricultural economy, proximity was a byproduct of the manufacturing economy and it made it easier for us to enjoy one another while we weren't at work.

Manufacturing was a way of life too. Third and fourth generation factory workers continued to work in factories that their parents and grandparents worked in. The day-to-day routines of manufacturing life were passed on through generations along with the traditions of everyday life – like bowling leagues – that were associated with the work.

Today, well over seventy percent of everything that America produces comes from the service sector. Unlike the concrete goods produced by farming and manufacturing, service work provides intangible goods like information. Additionally, personal computing allows service workers to work remotely and alone so fewer people interact regularly at work.

Service work is more often a job than a way of life. Most people that have service jobs have worked in multiple industries. Very few service workers are doing the same thing that their parents did. Even if they are, most industries and businesses have changed so dramatically that the work is quite different. For example, you may have worked in your father's hardware store as a child – an atmosphere that would have been rich with Simple Community. Today, if you are still in the hardware business, you are most likely part of a chain, and the store is probably significantly different. Although the changes may have taken place gradually, the end effect is that working for a chain does not naturally give rise to casual face-to-face conversations or traditions. Consequently, there are fewer opportunities to enjoy family and friends. We are gradually losing the contexts to gather.

You may not have realized that you were missing anything because we are still surrounded by people, but after 25 years of research and observation, it is clear to me: We need more of each other's company. We need more Simple Community. What is Simple Community? The following illustration comes directly from Living Simple Community.

The Backyard Barbeque: a story of Simple Community.

He didn't think about the good he was doing while he flipped burgers for a bunch of neighbors in his backyard. He never meant it as an act of building community. He just felt like being with his friends. He did intend to fix the wobbly leg on the picnic table before anyone got there, but he didn't get around to it.

The gathering was one of those magical moments when everything comes together: great weather, good times, and great conversation. Everyone there knew it was special and worth repeating.

Who would have thought that a leaning neighbor and a bowl of coleslaw would bond a neighborhood together for more than 20 years? They were all talking when the neighbor leaned on the table and the whole thing collapsed, leaving her sitting on the ground covered with coleslaw.

She hosted the neighbors a month later. Three brought big bowls of coleslaw. A tradition was born. Coleslaw continued to be served and its story was revived every time the neighbors gathered – the first Saturday of every summer month – just as it was the first time the picnic table collapsed.

Simple Community is

PEOPLE

taking TIME to gather together

in a PLACE suited to enjoying each other.

They bring the RESOURCES needed to have fun.

The best times give rise to STORIES that they tell again

and again. When they are really lucky, something happens

that creates a TRADITION, which begs to be repeated.

These are the six ingredients of Simple Community.

People who have the time to build Simple Community are the ones who kindle the fire. As long as you stick to small gatherings, like backyard barbecues, gathering as a group is relatively easy, but the bigger the group or activity becomes, the harder it is to organize. You start needing bigger places and more resources. Stories are the evidence that Simple Community lives. Traditions are small, silly things often born of completely unintended circumstances which happen at a time when people are doing things they love. It doesn't get much better than that. And it really is as easy as that.

Working with your family on the farm or with your neighbors in the factory made the logistics of a barbeque pretty simple. The people were already in the same place at the same time. All they had to do to support Simple Community was add the food. I remember all the things my parents' generation was involved in, like bridge clubs and bowling leagues. They were simple, regular events that friends and coworkers participated in.

How can we return to that simplicity? I had two goals when I wrote this book: to bring together the three groups of people who can make Simple Community possible and to encourage companies to shift ten percent of the $300 billion they spend on marketing, sales and advertising in America each year to support those community initiatives. The more the concepts of Building Simple Community are used and passed along, the sooner we could see significant investment in communities across America. Imagine how much could be done to support Simple Community with $30 billion dollars per year.

Chapters three through seven are intended primarily for marketers. They are about marketing trends, strategies and ideas for the future. American marketing is so dominated by advertising and is so focused on new, computer-based message delivery systems, that few marketers are considering building their businesses by enriching live experiences.

Chapters eight and nine are also for people with access to gathering places. Chapter eight provides a new way of thinking about community and chapter nine describes the work that has already been done in the NCAA and NFHS.

Chapter ten begins the discussion of scalable grassroots. I say beginning because it is my hope that this book, coupled with the work of the NCAA and NFHS in the last couple years, will bring scalable grassroots to reality. It will require cooperation, but it is possible now and it is the right thing to do.

CHAPTER 3

A New Way of Thinking

A changing paradigm

Stephen Covey's classic business book, The Seven Habits of Highly Effective People,[1] starts with a superb story of paradigm change. I will not do it justice, but it goes something like this: A business man was traveling home on the commuter train at the end of a long day when a father and his three sons came on board. The father let his kids run wild and did not quiet them or tell them to calm down. The business man was angry about the actions of the kids and the disregard of the father. He thought the father should be more sensitive and realize that everyone on the train was tired and as a courtesy he should get his boys under control. The father noticed the man's displeasure and approached him just before getting off the train. "I'm sorry for my boys," he said, "I know I should probably have done something, but we are just coming from the hospital where their mother died." Instantly the man saw the situation differently. By understanding the whole situation, he could reevaluate and understand what was more important. He experienced a paradigm shift. A paradigm shift is most likely to happen as result of a dynamic experience or from exposure to new information so compelling it requires us – forces us – to think another way.

I am not the first to suggest that the advertising and marketing industries in America are long overdue for a paradigm shift. My favorite take on the problem is Purple Cow by Seth Godin,[2] which chronicles the incredible success over the years of marketing through mass advertising followed by many examples of why that approach no longer works. I also appreciate Godin's proposed solution – to a point. He proposes that the way to break through to consumers is by creating remarkable brand stories. I would love that approach if I thought the solution was driven by what people need and do, but it is not. Godin leaves it for the brands to create stories

This new paradigm goes one step beyond that. The old marketing and advertising paradigm begins with the assumption that people have informational needs beyond their reach. That is no longer true. However, we do have a different need that we cannot fulfill on our own but that is met by Simple Community. The following summary of the new paradigm illustrates both the problem with the current model and the promise for a new view. Simply said, we need to shift the paradigm to:

- Think of individuals as PEOPLE, not consumers
- We get enough information and messages, we need more STORIES
- And the stories need to be THEIR stories, not the stories written by the brand

PEOPLE, not consumers

You are not a consumer. You are a person – a person who buys things. In the current consumerism paradigm, we are losing something that we need far more than the things we purchase. We need to be people, and we really want the activities we engage in to feel personal too. We may not need Bob's hardware anymore, but we sure do miss Bob. We lost Bob, the corner market, and the drug store with the soda fountain. Those weren't manifestations of consumerism; they were our friends, neighbors, and a part of life.

The personal connection to customers wasn't lost solely because service work began to dominate the economy. America used to have thousands of neighborhood hardware stores, drug stores, markets, dairies, lumber yards, and so on. They were all separate businesses, owned and run by locals. However, the ability to consolidate services has made it possible, and much more profitable, for one company to own hundreds and sometimes thousands of little stores.

Now, Americans very rarely purchase their necessities directly from their neighbors. The key word here is "directly." Millions of people work behind the scenes to support Wal-Mart, McDonald's, and BP gas stations across America. And those who do work the front line, entry-level cashiers and customer service representatives, are transient. As a brief illustration: I have a morning coffee routine. I have repeatedly grown fond of the employees and learned their names right before they move on to a new job.

The owners and employees of large companies and retail store chains are people who want more Simple Community too. Yes, even the owners, because in fact, the majority of stock for big companies is owned by everyday people. If you have stocks, a retirement fund, a 401k program, a savings account, or mutual funds, you probably own a piece of a major company. So YOU are an owner. Progress is good, but as a byproduct we no longer see how our purchases of goods and services continue to provide paychecks for our neighbors. Although we do support each other in our buying and with our work, it is no longer personal or community-centered.

What if you could go to work every day and think mostly about what would make life better for you as a person, not a consumer? What if that thinking made your life better and your work more successful? What if a significant chunk of the over $300 billion invested annually in American advertising and marketing could be reinvested in those things that really improved the quality of life for people while increasing sales?

STORIES, not messages

Although revolutionary thought and technological advancement have made us much more powerful, efficient and effective at selling things, we are operating on an outdated assumption. American needs have changed and our marketing approach and investment need to change as well. Advertising is still a powerful tool. The lack of cigarette advertisements is a great example. I can name neither the best selling nor the newest cigarettes. Even at its weakest, advertising highlights new products and those in crowded categories. But with literally over 100 million websites and the ability to use search engines like Google, do you really feel that there is a shortage of information about brands?

Technology is not the solution either. It is possible to think of digital marketing as the solution because people can participate in the message, but it's still advertising. It's still the delivery of largely unwanted messages. In this era we can, and do, seek out the information we need to make decisions about what we buy when we want that information.

This is not a crusade to end advertising. There is more than enough research to show that advertising increases sales. This is an argument for moderation and modest redirection. Technology has enabled the explosion of information from all angles. Building Simple Community provides an action plan to refocus a small portion of ad dollars on the natural fit between brands and the most important and enjoyable things that people do. This is a good investment approach for two reasons: When people are looking for a product the brand that provided them with an enjoyable experience will more likely be chosen, and the experience provides an added value to people's lives.

This is where stories come in. When you go out for the evening and the next day a co-worker asks how it went, you will say little if it was nothing special, maybe five words or less – or just a dismissive grunt. If you had a great time, you will describe it with a story: "It was great because..," or "It was so funny that..." Stories are proof of life, the proof that Simple Community has taken place.

Next time someone asks you about your life and you have time to think about your response, ask yourself whether you are getting everything you want and need out of life. No stories, no life. We need messages and information; we have access to them. We need stories more, but to get stories we need to be living an interesting life. Life leads to stories, and stories can bring life to your brand.

Their stories, not yours

I confess, I have developed ideas and then scripted an ad to show how it would look if it actually took place. You can probably think of several TV ads with similar story lines. The problem is, whether the ads are funny or touching, even those of us in the advertising industry rarely remember the brand. One reason that their impression is so fleeting is the sheer amount of advertising we consume. Another is that scripted stories rarely fit reality and we don't personally experience them, so they aren't internalized. Conversely, stories that come from authentic community experiences live on in people's memories. There is a way to provide people with memorable experiences and naturally include your product or service in a way that is valued and becomes part of the stories people tell. That approach is covered in chapter seven.

Why do we need a new way of thinking?

We are overwhelmed. Changes and new opportunities come at us constantly and we just don't have the ability to keep up, so we go with the "tried and true." Spending $300 billion a year in messages is too much. Especially because most of those messages are not just forgotten, but ignored. Stories from our own lives, – as people, not consumers – stick when messages don't.

CHAPTER 4

How Ads Became Unwanted Alarms

Companies need to change how they think before they will be willing to invest significantly in how their brands can enhance life. The time is right for that change. The role and value of advertising has changed and the amount of advertising is truly staggering. But the day of controlled mass media has ended and instead of using a new model, traditionalists are trying to merely extend the old model on new media.

How much is too much? When advertising was in its infancy, more than one hundred years ago, the need was clear. Everything was scarce. Advertising created awareness of products and brands, promoted their benefits, and connected people to buying opportunities. Before 1900, American brands spent over one billion dollars per year on advertising. The business has been big for a long time. So much has been invested in advertising that it has become an art form. But somewhere along the line the message became an alarm.

An alarm is intended to accomplish three things: 1) get you to stop thinking about what you are thinking about; 2) think about the alarm; and 3) as a result of the alarm, do something. The best and earliest alarms were designed to save lives. But now, with $300 billion in messages added to the constant alarms of cell phones, emails, junk mail, and instant messages– many of which are unwanted – all of us have formed sophisticated alarm avoidance systems. Our first response to nearly any message is "How do I avoid this?"

We are ignoring more than advertising alarms. One morning not long ago,

I was sitting in the Detroit airport. The terminal is literally a mile long and I was somewhere in the middle. I was eating a roll, drinking coffee, reading the paper and waiting to board my flight when every alarm on Earth went off. Lights, sirens, whooping things, voices, the whole works. Fire trucks were driving up to several of the ramps outside. This had to be the big one. Panic! Chaos!! People trampling over each other!!! Pandemonium!!!!

Got the picture? Well of course none of that – except the alarms – actually happened. Every element of the alarm part was true, complete with the fire trucks. But nobody, including myself, did anything differently. In spite of the sirens, flashing lights and fire trucks, people continued to board their planes. Our alarm defenses block out everything – even alarms designed to save our lives.

The alarming nature of marketing and advertising hit home for me several years ago when a friend asked me to help with a fundraising program for a non-profit organization. In the meeting, he told me the time was right for the fundraiser. When I asked why, he said his organization was hitting a quiet spell in their work when they could do it without taxing their resources. The timing was right for HIM. He hadn't thought about how the targets of his fundraising might feel. He didn't even know who they were. He just assumed that when he sent out a mailing or did a dinner program the people would come and the money would flow.

What a common mistake. I am certain you are not sitting around wondering when product "X" is coming out with their next ad because you just can't wait to see it. You are not sitting by the phone wondering when your third cousin's favorite charity is going to call you for a check. But when it comes time for us to create our marketing campaign or fundraiser we assume that everyone else is going to stop what they are doing to pay attention.

Alarms from the mass media era

It is not just that there are too many alarms. A big part of the problem is that most of the alarms were designed for the days of mass communication when messages were sent without the ability to provide feedback.

The end of the American mass media culture was unthinkable even in 1980. The media were assumed to have unstoppable power, much of it vested in the three broadcast networks. Mass communication made marketing simple and reach a given. In addition to the ability to use just three networks to reach everyone, mass media meant total control by the producers. Americans could neither alter nor respond to the communication they received. It was the best and simplest of times for advertisers and business. Both thrived.

The Internet killed the passive mass audience. Significant portions of the American population rarely gather at one point in time to watch the same program on TV. The NFL Super Bowl is the biggest but reaches less than half the nation. I Love Lucy did better than that every week in the early days of black & white television.

The death of mass put advertisers on notice and forced a change in business models for any media-based technology. For the first time in 2003, Americans paid more to receive media without commercials than brands paid to provide free programming with advertising. That same year was the first in which more advertising dollars were spent on non-traditional media than on TV and other traditional sources.

The traditionalists are trying to hang on by using new media combined with the out-dated, alarming approaches. New communication media for advertising and marketing presents two problems, though. The first, our unreasonable expectations of communication technology, is covered in more detail in Chapter Five of Living Simple Community. We assume personal computing can provide the answer to the lost value of traditional advertising. However, the mere fact that we have new technology does not mean that it is the answer. Our needs changed. We don't need more information – we need relationships and opportunities. We assume that because new media are the rage, they are also the answer. That's a problem.

The second problem is that marketers and advertisers are turning to the new media for "Social networking" and "media engagement" which are concepts created by them to try to capture some of the billions of dollars that companies are moving out of traditional advertising each year.

I don't think Americans are buying it. My telephone is neither "engaging" nor a "social network." It is a phone. It is a tool I have accepted as important in my life. It is a tool I use to reach people when I can't be with them in person. It is a medium – something in the middle. Media are tools between people when they can't be together. The PEOPLE engage. Their lives are social networks. A website is no more a social network than is the exchange of letters through the mail. At best, the Internet and communication technology provide us with a communication network. At best.

Just as there is still a need for advertising, new media technology is not useless for our purposes. It allows interaction. It provides a powerful and constant connection between people. Advertising and new media are not problems.

The problem is thinking that either one stands alone as the answer for future marketing. It would be equally wrong to think that supporting Simple Community, alone, is the answer.

The combination of real face-to-face experiences in Simple Community and the connective power of new media could be very effective. Instead of thinking of new media as the center of future marketing, imagine marketing programs that have been carefully developed to provide a powerful Simple Community experience at the heart of the strategy. Those experiences then provide genuine content fed into "social networking" sites. Those sites are not the heart, they are the veins and arteries that allow the understanding of Simple Community to flow throughout the country and spread the vision. The stories and videos go out. People reply with their stories and feedback which in turn leads to more experiences at the heart of the activity and the best is refined and repeated.

A wonderful example of that very thing can be found at www.diicommunity.org where the NCAA Division II schools are sharing the best-tested Simple Community ideas. The website was intended for the internal use of the 308 Division II schools. There has been no major promotional strategy – no alarms. In less than two years, over 350,000 visitors have visited the site to find out how to build and extend Simple Community. More is available about the NCAA Division II program in Chapter eight.

CHAPTER 5

The Three Intersections of Sales and Marketing

Marketers and advertisers spend a lot of time evaluating the benefits and characteristics of their products and services. They consider which messages best convey the most important values of their brands and the demographic characteristics of their core consumers. But how often do marketers and advertisers think about the lives of people as they encounter and use their products and services? That is, what ELSE is going on while people are hearing ads, browsing store shelves, and using products? Thinking about how a product or service lives in the midst of everything else taking place is at the heart of the new paradigm – thinking of how your brand fits into the stories of people and their lives.

This is an appeal to flip perspectives. Instead of starting by thinking about what your brand needs and attempting to engage consumers in ways that fit the brand agenda, start by thinking about "what else" is typically going on in the lives of people when their lives are most likely to intersect with your brand. A strategy built on this flipped perspective would start with research to understand "what else" goes on when people encounter the brand. It would continue with a survey to determine the most common "what else" conditions present when the product or service is used. The most common contexts would be observed in an experiential qualitative study to determine opportunities to enhance the story making ability of the brand. I have done all the above with products from bathroom cleaners (you would be surprised how many people wipe the rim and then wipe the seat) to blue jeans ("The closet is where clothes go to die.") and services from life insurance sales calls to the bedside manner of physicians. There are so many things people commonly do without giving much thought to the process.

There are three steps in moving toward a people-first approach to marketing. The first is knowing the three common points of intersection between brands and the lives of people. The second is understanding how people think about how they spend their time and how they actually spend it. Finally, you have to identify how your brand can become part of the story. That is discussed in Chapter Seven.

Three intersections

Let me suggest that the lives of people and the products and services that they buy intersect on three different occasions. These intersections are predictable times that a product or service is likely to enter the thoughts or actions of a person. The three intersections are the INFORMATION seeking – or advertising – intersection, the BUYING – or point-of-sale – intersection, and the CONSUMPTION intersection.

The heart of sales and marketing programs in the old paradigm focus on the information seeking and buying intersections. Marketers create messages to intersect with specific consumers at targeted times, identified by market research techniques that have been used for decades. Media companies then buy advertising time to intersect the highest concentration of the target consumer demographic. More recent strategies have applied the old research goal of targeted marketing to new media technologies by bundling Internet services in the hope that, through aggregation of intersections, brands can effectively reach the same size audiences that they used to reach through mass media.

Research and marketing strategies for influencing consumer decisions at point-of-sale have also become much more sophisticated and powerful in identifying the best options for product and incentive placement as well as understanding foot traffic patterns through stores so brands can increase the power of intersection of brand appeals at point-of-sale. Brands understand and execute powerfully within the information seeking and buying intersections. The same cannot be said of the third intersection.

The third intersection, where the product or service is used or consumed, is the only intersection that people control. It is the ideal intersection of brands and people's lives, because it is the one time the person – not the brand – chooses the context. It is THEIR intersection, not the brand's. The personal nature of the consumption makes it the heart of the new marketing paradigm. And yet, how many strategies do you know of that target the context in which a product is used? Brands invest heavily in getting people to know about them and their values (information seeking intersection) and to get people to purchase their products (buying intersection), but once it is bought, they assume their brand has gotten all the possible value out of the intersection. American brands do not see the potential marketing value in the intersection of people's lives and their use of brands. The irony here is how much attention is given to customer satisfaction. The vast majority of research questions about customer satisfaction are brand-centered, not person centered. It's like the old joke about the self-centered person who, upon finishing a long story about himself, said to his friend "…but enough about me, how about you? What do you think about me?"

American social experience has become task oriented and impersonal. So little of what we do is built on intentionally supporting family and friends. So much of what it takes to maintain life is done through lifeless transactions. That just was not true 100 years ago. It doesn't have to be true today. We can have the best of efficient transactions and still invest in the quality of people's lives by starting to value the intersection of our brands at the point of use.

I will assume that your brand is getting great value out of the information seeking and buying intersections and will therefore focus my attention on the consumption intersection. But first, I want to point out the subtle migration of the consumption concept. In writing about the new paradigm, I suggested that we need to look at people as people, not as consumers. Once we see them as people – see their lives and what else they do while they interact with brands – then we can appreciate the importance of their consumption of our products and services. Their lives are not defined by what they consume. Their lives are defined by… their lives, and consumption is but one small part of life.

People, their time, and what they do

Let me suggest that there are several parts of life: working, sleeping, chores, school – these are all things that we have to do to support life. Whatever we do when we are not supporting life is truly living; we do all those other things because they allow us to enjoy our remaining free time in the way we choose. The things we do in our free time are the source of our greatest joys. We do not live to work; we work, go to school, eat, and do almost everything else, for the rare opportunities to enjoy ourselves in the ways that we choose.

During the past three decades, I have conducted several studies on how Americans choose to spend their free time. Among the more surprising findings is that Americans have much more free time than they realize. They believe they have 1-2 hours per day when in reality the average American has more than six free hours per day – over 40 hours per week. The perceived difference can be partially explained by the additional free hours most Americans have on weekends. But even taking the weekends into consideration, most Americans have twice as much free time during the week as they realize.

I discovered something quite powerful in the process of doing this research. People make their decisions according to how busy they think they are, whether they actually are busy or not. One person may have an average of six unscheduled hours per day but feel pressed for time, while someone else may have only two hours free and feel like they have all the time in the world. When it comes to how we spend free time, perception is reality. People act on what they believe to be true and set their priorities and make their time commitments accordingly.

At the end of this writing session, I will go to a play and dinner with my wife and friends. The decision to go out varies extremely by whether I feel pressure to finish writing by a certain time or whether I feel way ahead. A commitment to any recreational activity is far more invested for someone who feels they have little time than someone who believes they have all the time in the world. The time-poor person is committing what they believe to be a rare resource so he or she will be more selective and probably have higher expectations for the value of the time spent. A person who is time-rich feels there is less at stake – so less to lose if the experience is disappointing – because the activity is just another thing to do in a life filled with time.

The marketing approach for reaching people who feel they have little free time should be completely different than the approach taken with those who believe they have ample free time. With the time-poor person, you look for one very specific activity designed to appeal to something you know they care about. You personalize that experience for them and do everything you can to remove wasted time in the process. You invest less per activity targeted to the time-rich person and instead, develop repeating activities like sports leagues, bridge clubs or book groups.

But I am getting just a little ahead of myself. Whether a person actually has a little or a lot of free time, or whether he thinks he has a little or a lot, one thing is for sure: his free time is his own. No matter what he chooses to do, the point is this: he gets to choose. Free time is, without a doubt, THE part of life that gives rise to the richest stories. They are personal, meaningful stories because they come from time spent doing what we love the most.

My research of American free time and Simple Community[3] has allowed me to identify eight contexts or buckets of what people do in their free time. After many years I cannot find one free time activity that falls outside these buckets. I have studied the amount of time spent on each bucket, their priority, the favorite bucket(s), the desire for more time per bucket, and how they link together.

The eight contexts (buckets) of free time

Time with family and friends: No matter how I measure it, time with family and friends has always been the favorite, the top priority, the most desired. It has also been the one thing more people say they need more. Time with family and friends mostly about being together, the actual activity is fairly irrelevant. However, when the places and resources to do more with our family and friends are available to us we tend to take advantage of them.

Outdoor activity: This includes time in a park, running, fishing, biking, camping, gardening, hunting, bird watching and more.[4] Forty percent of all Americans say outdoor activity is important to them. While the priority of all the other buckets varies by age, people love outdoor activity from cradle to grave.

Personal time: We don't use all of our free time for socializing. People enjoy spending time alone. The three most common personal time activities are reading, time on the computer (not work/school related), and playing video games. By the way, video games are not just for kids. Popularity extends to age 48.

Productive leisure: Anything people do that produces something – intrinsic or extrinsic – is considered productive leisure. Examples include hobbies, classes for purposes other than work or formal education, volunteerism, political and religious activity, and many more.

Participation in exercise or sports activities: Not all sports fans play or exercise. Not all those who play are fans. The younger a person is, the more likely he is to be active.

Sports fan activity: This includes watching games or events on TV, attending competitions, following sports in the media, participation in fantasy leagues, and so on.

Watching TV other than sports: Because sports events on TV are usually live, they are quite different than other TV programs. People with a lot of free time spend most of it in this bucket.

Out-on-the-town: If we decided to get together on a Friday evening you would be surprised if I showed up with a bucket and sponges expecting to wash my car. You would not be surprised if I suggested coffee, dinner, a show, a party, or something similar. We have a bucket for getting together that covers a set of expectations for what people do when they "go out" together. Not surprisingly, out-on-the-town peaks between the ages of 18-24, even surpassing interest in sports for the males during those years. As we age the desire and activity declines.

I have found from my own research that it is possible to understand all the other things – the "what else" – that our marketing competes with, at least to an extent. Using the eight buckets, I can identify the dominant contexts of people who use a product or service. I also find distinctive "what else" differences between users of different brands. Having identified the one to three buckets most associated with "what else" behavior I do deeper survey work to get a prioritized list of activities within each bucket. I observe the product use and "what else" behaviors that have the greatest potential for stimulating stories worth telling. Then I consider what could be done to provide experiences that will lead to those stories. That thought process is detailed in Chapter 7.

New paradigm research – looking at people rather than consumers – is actually already in use by research and design teams, just not for marketing purposes. But here again, they rarely think about the life of people. They think about the product or the process of the service – much like the measurement of customer satisfaction. In fact, I have a million dollar idea for you. I did a study once on why males don't do housework. Hand a six foot tall guy a broom and you will have part of your answer. It's too short. All handles are designed for shorter people. If you made a broom only a tall guy could use, who knows what would happen. At minimum, you would eliminate one more "what else" that keeps tall guys from doing housework.

Once you are armed with an understanding of people's time use and contexts, you can turn your attention to the experiences that will ignite stories for your brand.

CHAPTER 6

From Messages to Experiences

Sports and experiential marketing: near misses

Let's review for a moment.

- It is not as easy for Americans to spend enjoyable time together because of our change to a service based economy.

- Americans want to spend more enjoyable time together with their family and friends.

- Companies spend over $300 billion per year to sell their products and services in America alone.

- An overwhelming part of the investment is in messages that have become unwanted alarms.

- New technology has changed the way people get information and the way they choose to learn about – or avoid – information about products and services.

- There is a new way to think about how we sell:

- PEOPLE, not consumers,

- STORIES, not messages,

- THEIR stories, not the brand's stories

- There are three points of intersection between the lives of people and products and services they buy and use:

- The information seeking – advertising – intersection

- The buying – point-of-sale – intersection

- The consumption intersection

- Traditional marketing and advertising has put all its weight on the information and buying intersections. There is a great opportunity in the consumption intersection.

- In the new approach to marketing, we have an opportunity to have an impact on what is most meaningful to people by focusing on the time they use products and services. Investing in experiences, especially in Simple Community, opens the door to heart-felt stories that include your brand and at the same time actually improve the social context of America.

You may be tempted to say "Isn't that what I am doing with sports marketing?" I would like that to be true. But a closer look at how sports and other forms of experiential marketing came into being suggests that we are far from getting the most out of our investment in experiences.

There is a simple way to see whether your experiential programs use the old or the new paradigm. Ask yourself what the stated objectives are? In most cases, the goals are either to distribute a specific message, build awareness or favorability, or align a product attribute with an experiential attribute – any brand with "ice" in the title sponsors hockey. These are all examples of information intersections. If the objective is sampling or testing a product, your experience is supporting the buying intersection. In the last decade, brands have increasingly articulated their usage objectives. They want the majority of people at the event to be drinking their beverage, eating their food, or wearing their clothes. That objective is an attempt to link the use of the product with events that naturally call for their products. That is a step in the right direction. Unfortunately, the number of those events that people attend leaves a considerable amount of reach to be desired.

Doesn't it seem wiser to support an experience or activity that takes place several times per week or even every day? Short of that, an activity that creates a personal story that will be told again and again would have pretty good returns as well. When you think of your current experiential marketing, how often do you accomplish one, or both, of those things? How often is your engagement with an experience impacting everyday use or producing a story that will be told again and again?

It feels like we are getting closer to developing powerful experiential marketing programs. However, we are backing into it. We are trying to apply old paradigms designed to deliver mass messages to experiences that have the potential to have profound lasting impact, one person at a time. Here is why that approach is backwards:

The most established part of experiential marketing is sports marketing. Companies have promoted and supported sports in America for over 100 years. For all but the past 30, that support has been more philanthropy than business. In 1996 I started suggesting in my presentations at conferences and companies that the sports industry was probably "born" in 1980. I said that with the intention of starting a debate. I was hoping for people working in sports to realize the starting point of sports as a business industry and to begin a rallying cry for adopting the better, and more mature, business practices of real industries. Nobody ever picked up the debate, because so many dynamic things happened around that time to support the logic of my argument.

Why 1980?

- ESPN started in 1979, providing dramatically expanded shelf space for sports content on television.

- The USA hockey gold medal in the 1980 Olympics was a national celebration unlike any other, suggesting that sports were close to the heart of America's social identity.

- Anheuser-Busch created Busch Media Group in 1980, the first company to integrate their media spending with the group that managed sports involvement. The resulting leverage of media buying and the sports property rights negotiation process literally changed sponsorship.

- In 1980, NIKE and other footwear and sports apparel companies were on the way to becoming the dominant casual fashion in America, proving the profitability of sportswear.

- The NBA was breaking as another major sport first with Magic Johnson and Larry Bird, then with Michael Jordan, proving the marketability of stars.

- The profitable 1984 LA Olympics changed the way we thought about the Olympic movement from that time on.

All these experiences demonstrated the financial power of sports in America.

They did not, however, get an industry started or cause the leaders from a broad range of sports entities to work together to build that industry. We backed into the financial success. There were tremendous opportunities to make money and more than enough courageous people to attempt to meet the appetite Americans had for seemingly anything having to do with sports.

There are problems with backing into an industry. Any time you back in, you are walking and looking backwards. If you walk backwards, you don't see what is ahead. In the case of sports, business people just kept building new games, leagues, products, and apparel without thinking about when a threshold would be reached. At some point, you back into a wall. There comes a time when there is little or no more growth potential.

We were walking backwards. We weren't looking at what was coming in front of us. I was stunned in 1988 when CBS lost hundreds of millions of dollars in one year on their MLB contract. I was teaching at Temple University at the time and put half a dozen doctoral students to work to find the financial metrics CBS used to arrive at a value that could have been that far off. There were none. In 1988 there was not one piece of ongoing substantial research to measure sports interest and activity in America.

Until I started the ESPN Sports Poll in 1994, it was not possible to know how many NFL fans were also fans of the NBA. By default, leagues sold their value as if an NFL fan were a fan of only the NFL. In fact, the typical American is a fan of 6 sports and an avid fan of two or three. Why is that important to know? We can't say we are walking forward unless we know what we are competing against. Would you create a new shoe company without knowing about the need and demand for more new shoes?

We are backing into the sports industry although it is not yet mature. There is a restaurant industry, a soft drink industry, a quick service restaurant industry, and a hundred more. In mature industries, there are common operating practices. Product lines are similar, pricing structures are similar, production and packaging have uniform characteristics. All those practices increase the efficiency of companies who service the industry. If you are a marketer and you switch jobs within the industry, you can safely assume that the required knowledge and the processes to do your new job will be similar. That is not the case in sports. Every major sports league or organization has a completely different approach to the way they do business. Obviously, their seasons are different. But think about the variation in marketing deals:

- Sport A requires you to pay a fee to use their marks throughout the nation, AND you must buy a certain amount of advertising.
- Sport B has no media requirement, but you can't use national marks within 75 miles of a team if you don't have team rights.
- College sports deals are different at every school, AND you have to do deals with a conference and the NCAA.

Unified industries such as television, in which advertising rates are determined the same way for all the networks, make it abundantly clear how far the sports industry is from becoming unified. Which moves me to another problem: The development of sports – and other forms of experiential marketing – is backward. The way we THINK about experiential marketing is looking backward. I am back to the old paradigm again.

Before sports were businesses, before 1980, there was little, if any, business expectation from investments in sports and other experiences. More often than not, the decision to be involved in experiences came from senior leadership, who pulled the money to pay for it from multiple sources without assigning bottom-line responsibilities to an individual unit. Sometimes, experiences were managed by corporate communications or even a company foundation.

Increasingly, since 1980, sports funding has come from marketing, brands or advertising and with an expectation that the investment would lead to profits. How did we get there, and how does that translate into looking backward? From 1980 on, examples of sports producing huge profits were common. Go back to the list of things that happened or started around 1980 for a reminder. It was only logical to think that if leagues, teams, players, clothing and shoes could make money from sports, then all sports involvement should be profitable.

The problem was that we looked backward to figure out what we should do with sports. We looked to what had worked for decades. We expected sports and other experiences to produce the same value as television advertising and point-of-sale displays. We expected a mass intersection of information and buying from a highly personal and singular experience.

Where ten or twenty years earlier there were no expectations for a return on investment (ROI), by 1990 the cost of sponsorship involvement and experiential marketing was substantial enough to look for returns. Sports, entertainment, experiential, and integrated marketing units were developing in companies, but while every company has a line for legal fees, advertising, insurance and the like, few have substantial line items for sports or experiential marketing. Experiential costs are still often covered in marketing, sales, promotion, and advertising budgets.

I just recently had a conversation with a marketing executive in a major American company. We were talking about the importance of investing in Simple Community and, by extension, experiential marketing. He told me that if there was a solid measure of ROI, he would have no problem getting the company to invest. He said his company can predict with confidence the increase in sales for every dollar they spend in advertising. Then he asked me if there were ROI measures like that for Simple Community. There are not. Not yet anyway. There will be soon.

I thought about that conversation for a long time. I realized why we don't have – and won't for some time – solid ROI numbers for Simple Community and experiential marketing. First, we don't invest much in experiences. My goal with this book is to move American investment in Simple Community to 10%. Imagine for a minute 90% of all marketing dollars were invested in Simple Community and only 10% in advertising. What do you think the ROI would look like for advertising? Not so good. Simple Community would be robust and helpful to society. Advertising would be too small to measure. It will take courage – and that courage is coming – for American companies to invest the appropriate tens of millions of dollars in American life experiences. I have seen it happen. There are products that have overtaken others because one brand spent tens of millions of dollars enhancing life experiences with the brand. It worked. They know it, which is why I can't tell you about it.

The second ROI problem goes back to sports being a relatively new industry with a disintegrated business model. Experiential marketing is not currently a standard part of American business. The media buying process is fairly uniform which makes transactions easier. With advertising, there is a way to measure what you are getting for each dollar through television ratings and other reach measures. All in all, it is pretty easy to use advertising and brands have an excepted system for measuring the value.

The same cannot be said for marketing through live experiences such as sports. Because no two sports leagues offer the same package, it is virtually impossible to compare the value of one sport to another. The ESPN Sports Poll is a solid measure of fan bases for more than two-dozen sports, but there is not a uniformly accepted measure of ROI, so brands don't have a standard measure of value for the dollar invested.

Even with minimal investment and lack of uniform measurement, with sports and live experiences, the problem is not with the ROI measures. They are just fine. The problem is with the assumptions regarding the value of experiential marketing in the first place. The problem is that we are stuck in the old paradigm of trying to use brand messages to reach consumers instead of building life experiences that foster stories from the lives of people that show appreciation for brand investment in life.

Let me illustrate.

Let's say I have a really big back yard and I want to put in a garden. I take off the grass and realize the dirt underneath is not very rich, so I need to pick up top soil before planting the garden. At first I think I can get by with a few bags. So I go to the store in my car, get the dirt, bring it home and put it on the patch of ground that will become the garden. Then I realize I need more dirt, a lot more, maybe hundreds of bags. In fact, not even bags, maybe just tons of dirt.

At that point I rightly figure my car is not the right vehicle to haul the dirt. I need something bigger. I suppose, if I wanted to, I could haul the dirt in the trunk of a limousine. After all, a limo is considerably larger than a normal car. I could probably haul quite a bit of dirt compared to a sub-compact car or a five gallon pail. And that, of course, would be backing into the problem.

Backing myself into an even bigger corner, I can even measure quite precisely the amount I haul and the cost per pound of hauling. As long as I compare the limo to a pail or small car, the ROI measure will be quite favorable for the trunk of the limo.

However, as soon as someone tells me there is such a thing as a dump truck, the ROI measures no longer work. The trunk of a limo isn't even on the charts compared to a dump truck.

And that is exactly what is happening in experiential marketing. We are backing into it. We are hauling dirt in the trunk of a limo. We are not even thinking about the best use of a limo. And the way we are using it will make it less attractive and less valuable for its intended use.

Here is the point of the illustration. Limos are like experiences. They are vehicles that are designed to take a small group of people to a wonderful place in comfort. A lot of married people have wonderful stories about the limo ride on their wedding day. Advertising is like a dump truck. One message can be presented with incredible tonnage through mass and new media. But you wouldn't want to take your friends to a party in a dump truck.

The purpose of experiences is the creation of personal stories that last a long time, stories created by individuals having wonderful experiences. Over 400 sponsor banners in a stadium is dirt in the trunk of a limo. It is trying to get a mass benefit out of an intimate experience.

We need to think in a new paradigm. Looking forward, thinking ahead, we can create and support wonderful Simple Community stories that are remembered long after ads are forgotten. You need tonnage for an ad to persist. You need one experience for a story. The ad is an alarm. The story is proof that life, including your brand's role in it, is happening.

Here is still another perspective on the powerful ROI potential of Simple Community. I recently saw some fascinating research on the importance of commitment to a brand versus loyalty.[5] The researchers said loyalty means: to this moment I have continued to use this product. Loyalty does not mean I won't change my mind tomorrow. And in fact their research showed "loyal" buyers do change. Committed shoppers do not change. Something has happened beyond the typical brand experience that translated into a commitment. If committed buyers can't get their specific brand they will search elsewhere or buy nothing. Interestingly, most of the indicators of commitment they used examined messages, not experiences. By default, their assumption is that the value of advertising builds commitment because they were measuring the product of advertising: messages. Their research, while interesting and promising, wasn't producing powerful results. Do people form commitments because of messages? Do you?

Maybe sometimes. But I have a strong suspicion that life experience has much more to do with causing commitments than do messages. Actually, when messages cause change or commitment they are often unintentional. Here is an example from my life. I bet it sparks one or more from your own.

When I was a teen in the 1960s I played drums in rock bands. For the times and under the circumstances the bands I played in did pretty well. Growing up in Ann Arbor, we played at a lot of college parties. We played at several of the after-game dances and proms at high school. I made enough money playing in bands that I was able to buy a car before I was old enough to drive.

My parents were very supportive of my musical efforts and allowed us to practice in our basement. One evening in the middle of practice I came up for a glass of water. Out of the blue my mom said, "I know you are going to use drugs." I was furious. I was so angry I couldn't speak. I never forgot that she said that. I was so upset that, to spite my mother, I decided to never do drugs of any kind… I'd show her…

I was probably 14 at the time. The years passed. I never did any recreational drug of any sort – not even a joint without inhaling. When I was in my thirties and the parent of two girls I was discussing parenting with my mom when somehow the issue of tough problems like drugs came up. I remembered what my mom had said many years before and figured I was certainly past the danger zone. It was time to confront her. "Mom, you remember when you told me you were sure I would use drugs? Well I didn't!" Her response – "I never said that…" As near as we could tell, she never did. We were both pretty sure I misunderstood what she said. It would have been completely out of character for my mom to have said it in the first place – even more so as a line out of the blue.

I never did drugs. I played in rock bands with guys who did – some died of overdoses. But I never even experimented. I was committed because of a message I MISUNDERSTOOD. We constantly try to change people with our words, but it seems so rare that our attempts have any impact. The unintended word or interpretation of a message seems more likely to cause change than its direct intention. The incredible, un-utilized, un-measured, and powerful value of experiential marketing comes from action. Actions indeed speak louder than words, and experiential marketing has more power than messages to achieve its intended result.

Messages rarely intentionally cause commitment. Experiences in life do. Delivering those experiences is the purpose of experiential marketing. Good news: experiences that bring commitment can be done on purpose.

CHAPTER 7

Remarkable Experiences

Remarkable Experiences:

Your first successful bike ride was a Remarkable Experience. It changed the rest of your life. The odds are pretty good you remember that first time, totally unintentionally. Having a baby is a Remarkable Experience. No parent – mother or father – ever forgets the birth of a child and his or her life is forever transformed by the experience. Most Remarkable Experiences have four characteristics:

- They change the person's life
- They are never forgotten
- They produce stories that the person enjoys telling and repeats
- They have an emotional connection.

Given the example above, it is easy to see how commitment is often born of a Remarkable Experience. But how is that of any benefit to a brand? People buy things they need or want. If it is a true need, life cannot go on without it. The strongest of our desires probably began with a positive experience with the product or service. In that case, product sampling – which is very definitely an experience, not a message – can be a Remarkable Experience.

Many people have a favorite restaurant. How does that come to be? Someone goes to a restaurant once and has a Remarkable Experience. It is so good that he comes back again and again. The restaurant becomes part of his life and in becoming part of his life, changes it. There was no message; it was born from an experience. Most people who have a favorite restaurant can tell you the name of the restaurant immediately and what they like about it. In other words, they have a story.

Building Simple Community – and your brand – with Remarkable Experiences

Apart from the discussion of how to build Simple Community, you can apply the following simple steps to build commitment through experiential marketing in any part of life.

Here is how it looks in Simple Community.

1. Think of the people who are most likely to want or need your product. Determine which of the eight categories of free time activity those people enjoy the most.

2. Identify how your brand meets a need or fulfills a desire within that category, which would make Simple Community easier, more accessible, or more fulfilling.

3. Identify the places where you can introduce your brand in a Simple Community experience that meets your brand's identified need or desire.

4. Provide BOTH the opportunity to be in that place and your brand as the solution.

As a result, your brand becomes part of the Remarkable experience. The best of these Remarkable Experiences happen in social settings and in Simple Community. What follows are some examples of Remarkable Experiences. Not everything that we do is about community or being with other people, so the final examples are unrelated to a social setting.

It could have been: The Great American Picnic

For ten points, which American president was famous for conducting fireside chats? If you said FDR you were right. Enough of us knew the answer to that question to illustrate the power of that experience. Roosevelt began the practice during the depression – before he was president… more than seventy years ago. Yet, we still remember.

The presidential candidates spent over $1 billion on advertising in 2008. Can you remember their messages? What do you think would help the new president when it comes time for re-election: a billion dollars of messages that have been completely forgotten, or the heritage of something like the fireside chats? The creation of a needed American heritage almost happened as part of the 2008 election. I firmly believe that the only reason it didn't happen was that there wasn't enough time.

I am writing this section of the book in June, 2008. Senators McCain and Obama are the presidential candidates. We have had a tough year in America, mortgage and banking problems, $4 gas, and the complete loss of discretionary spending dollars for most Americans. Right now, restaurants are feeling the impact of lost discretionary spending the most. We are eating out less often. This would be a wonderful time to spark Simple Community through picnics. We still need to eat. The use of a local park is free. It takes very little additional cost to turn a regular meal into a picnic. And picnics are a great way to enjoy Simple Community.

To provide resources to make picnics even more accessible and to encourage Americans to go out and have a picnic, I developed a program called "The Great American Picnic." I tried to get one of the candidates to fund the program. It had several elements:

- Neither candidate was saying much that demonstrated his appreciation of the real pain Americans felt due to their lack of cash for free time activities. The Great American Picnic would allow a candidate to say: "We know you are hurting, we know you are eating out less, but you still need to eat. Pack a picnic and go to the park."

- The Great American Picnic would have been a legacy for the candidate/president. It would have demonstrated that he related to people's hurt in the same way that FDR's fireside chats did during the depression.

- During the campaign the candidate would show up at one picnic each week. If elected, he would continue monthly picnics in America throughout his term.

- State party candidates would hold picnics at MiLB stadiums and share the story of natural desire for community demonstrated by the attendance growth of MiLB without marketing.

- A grill manufacturer actually agreed to provide 10,000 to 25,000 great grills to those people who have proven they do things to build community – in other words to YOU, the readers of this book. Part would be reward and thanks, part would be encouragement to extend, if ever so slightly, your community experience.

I firmly believe it was only a timing issue. We didn't know who the candidates would be until June. The total loss of discretionary spending couldn't have been predicted early enough either. We ran out of time.

The Great American Picnic would have been accomplished for less than ½ of one percent of what the candidates spent on advertising.

Building homes in the after-math of Katrina

Here is another example. Katrina created an opportunity for a lot of people to do some very good things. The company I was working for at the time decided against a holiday party and flew to New Orleans to work on houses that were part of Habitat for Humanity. It felt like any other day while riding the buses from the hotel to the worksites – complete with laughter even at the early hour. As we rode into the destroyed neighborhood everyone was silent, shocked. There are so many words… but none came out of anyone's mouth. We worked so hard that day and with such purpose. We worked with the realization that soon a family would live there. Each nail mattered. Katrina was no longer something that happened to "them." Working in the middle of New Orleans, we realized that "we" had all suffered a loss here. "They" had become a part of "us," and we of them.

Another group had worked at the same worksite the week before. They brought new tools and left them behind as a gift. They were DeWalt tools. I remember thinking that if DeWalt had been the ones to provide the tools they would have won commitment from me that day. They did not. And yet the power of experience is so great. Someone else provided DeWalt tools as a resource in a Remarkable Experience and DeWalt gets the halo in this book. Try doing that with an ad.

Brands can think of ways to make life better. It is okay to be intentional in creating Remarkable Experiences. In fact, that is one major point of this book. Start – FIRST – by thinking of the real needs and desires that have to be fulfilled for people to get more out of their free time and match them with what your brand delivers. Genuinely lead with a desire to contribute to what people do in their free time and you will be rewarded with commitment. Intentional Remarkable

Experiences (IRE) have the same four characteristics as other Remarkable Experiences but with modifications.

Teaching a child how to ride a bike

Teaching a child how to ride a bike is a Remarkable Experience. It becomes an IRE when a bike company creates a program for teaching that includes advice on safety. An even more thoughtful and powerful IRE is achieved with tips for how to capture the first moment on video tape. Even better, bike companies have enough experience to know when that moment is imminent. "When you see your child...." Had I known when the moment was at hand, I might have pictures today. I do not.

Maybe the parent's package for teaching a kid to ride a bike has already been done. It sure wasn't there when I was teaching my kids and therefore, I have no pictures. I still have the memory. Come to think of it, this has IRE potential for a camera company as well.

The bike company that can teach me to teach my kid will be the bike company that gets my business. Today, if I had the video of that first bike ride because of the XYZ Bike Company's parents bike program, every time I saw or showed that video I would think positively of them and mention that they are the reason I have the video. Additionally, because it was a safer experience for my daughter because of XYZ's tips, I would also mention that they cared about the safety of my child. After all that, is there any doubt about brand of bikes I would buy for the rest of my life?

A million trees

Here is an example of an IRE that is not related to Simple Community. XYZ Lumber, a national lumber producer has had a distant relationship, at best, with the public. They have also had bad press lately about alleged unfriendly environmental practices. Most people that plant a tree form a bond with it, especially if it is a high quality tree that commemorates someone or something. So XYZ decided to create Remarkable Experiences by planting one million trees in America to transform the impression of the company.

A storm hit a town in the Midwest and knocked down 10,000 mature trees. Bob lost seven trees in his yard alone. One week after the storm Bob got a nice card from XYZ with a list of trees – oaks, maples – good trees known to grow well in his city. XYZ asked Bob to pick seven trees and suggested he dedicate each to someone he loved. The trees were delivered, with easy and clear instructions for planting and care, within a month, at no additional charge. They were beautiful trees, each with sturdy, enduring remembrance ribbons. Bob never stopped appreciating those trees, and every time someone asks about the ribbons he gladly tells the story about how XYZ thought of him after the storm.

So I ask again, which would you rather have, the million forgotten ads or 200,000 people with your trees telling the story of your company as their trees grow for years to come?

Where do IREs come from? Several sources
■ *The IRE catalog*

Ever since I figured this out I started looking for the kinds of events that have potential for Remarkable Experiences. As you will discover, the first time you do most things, it is Remarkable. But some turn out to be more memorable than others. For example, only half of people remember their first bike ride, but every parent who taught their child remembers when their children first rode away. Nearly everyone remembers their first kiss. Not so many remember the first day of school. Many IRE candidates are personal, most have a social component. So far, I have just fewer than 1,000 candidate IREs in the catalog.

■ *Opportunity-defined IREs*

When you are looking for IREs that build Simple Community, the easiest way to be sure they will be remarkable is if they have already happened. For example, Hurricane Katrina, although it was remarkable in a negative way, had a lasting impact on people's lives. If you associate your brand with experiences that relate to the hurricane, you can be sure that the memory will also be remarkable, as with my experience with DeWalt tools. Listen when community-hearted people come to you with an experience suggestion that fits your brand. If they feel the need in their communities and are coming to you for resources, they are bringing you the best possible research. If one person feels a need that is strong enough to warrant reaching out for help, you can be sure that providing resources will leave a lasting impression in many people's hearts.

Starting with an experience, think of the many products and services that could enhance people's free time. Whether they reduce the cost or add to the experience, there are usually several products and services that can be associated with experiences that are already remarkable.

■ Brand-defined IREs

The final approach to building IREs is through a needs/desire analysis by a product, service or brand. Be careful not to get trapped in a message tactic. The goal is not to say something with your brand, it is to do something. Think beyond why you want to sell it. Think of the people's lives. Their story. Think of a desire or need for your brand, but think of it from the perspective of an individual, not a consumer's or a shopper's experience.

The key is stories. When people ask Bob about the ribbons on his trees, he mentions XYZ lumber, not because of the company's goal to be the leading provider of home construction lumber, but because of his own seven special trees. When parents mention the bike company that provided them with an educational video, they aren't taking the company's revenue goals into account, they are relaying their appreciation of a program that made a difference in their lives. By looking beyond the consumer, companies can find a human need that they are able to meet that will reward them with more than purchase: Brand ambassadors, committed to buying their products and sharing positive stories about their brand.

In case you are not convinced, here is a story about how I inadvertently became a brand ambassador. In July, 2008, I was stuck for six hours in the Philadelphia Airport with a co-worker. You can talk about a lot in six hours. Being stuck in an airport naturally gives rise to the topic of traveling. We got around to a common contemporary American history question, "Where were you on 9/11?" I was in south Florida. My co-worker was in Atlanta. As chance would have it, both of us had rented cars from Hertz. At the time, I figured right away that nobody would be flying very soon. The most important thing at that moment was to get back home to Michigan to be with my family. Although I was supposed to have returned the car later that day, I decided not to call Hertz and just start driving. I realized in the back of my mind that I might end up paying $500 or even $1,000 for that decision, but at that point cost was not a priority.

It took me two days to get home. I will never forget what happened when I returned the car at a small local Hertz desk in a hotel in Ann Arbor on September 13th. They charged me something like $20 a day for the two extra days. That was it. Hertz had essentially "forgiven" everyone and decided it was more important for people to get home than for the company to get extra money. My co-worker from Atlanta told nearly the same story.

Here is what is important about our Hertz stories.

1. "Their story, not yours." This was not a marketing story. It was not made up. It didn't come from a creative or strategy department, it came from my own experience.

2. "Stories, not messages." It was a story of a company – Hertz – realizing their potential to positively affect their consumers' lives.

3. "Never forgotten." Almost seven years later we are still telling the story.

4. "Including the brand." We clearly remember that Hertz was the company that was so good to us when we needed them, and

5. "With appreciation." It is a positive brand memory.

I don't know how much money they "lost" in revenue by forgiving everyone, but how much would Hertz have to spend in advertising to have people still telling such a positive story – now included in a book – seven years later?

There have been several books in recent years that talk about the power of stories. I found two in particular – All Marketers Are Liars by Seth Godin,[6] and Made to Stick by Chip & Dan Heath[7] – to be very useful in providing advice for how to build ideas or stories with power. But there is a huge difference between building or making up great stories and living great lives that produce great stories. Simple Community cannot be built on fantasy or ideas. It must be the real deal.

Think of the stories you tell in your life and how often you tell stories. One of the things I love most about my wife Vicki is her story telling. I love going out with her or having friends over because I know – regardless of the setting – she will have a great story to tell and everyone will love it. Great story telling is one part how you tell it and ten parts living a life rich in experiences that produce stories. Vicki has at least twenty parts rich life. She has so many interests and makes the absolute maximum out of her free time. As if that's not enough, she is always starting something new. Her life is a constant source of stories that arise naturally from all the valuable and enjoyable things she does.

As with people and traditions, stories can't be forced. If the effort is spent on enjoying free time, the stories will come. You don't shape people's free time or communities with stories. Rather, you can get a great sense of how your building is going by listening for stories. If there are none, something is missing. If there are stories, they will tell you what they value the most and give you clues for what to invest more resources in to increase the richness of your activities.

Stories also help to welcome others to your experiences by illustrating what is at the heart of your community, instead of the process and ingredients. When you buy a car you don't go to a show room and see a bunch of parts on the floor, you see the whole car. They don't show you how the car is put together, they let you drive. You buy a car for the experience, not for the parts and the process. Community is about the whole thing – it is made up of infinite little parts that all come together to create one wonderful experience.

CHAPTER 8

The Importance of "Places" for Simple Community

At the heart of wonderful experiences are the places where people gather. There are literally millions of gathering places in America. The vast majority of them are being used for something other than Simple Community. With very little effort, most could also facilitate opportunities to gather.

Here comes another paradigm shift. This one is not as much for marketing or business people as for those who work in jobs where people gather.

What if schools were always open the same way factories are? What if America had one-third as many school buildings and every school had three shifts of students and a different set of teachers for each shift? What if kids went to school year-round and graduated from high school when they were 14 and college when they were 17?

Relax.

That is not what I am suggesting.

But the fact is that the real estate resources exist to do that very thing. The places to teach are always there, whether we use them or not. So are the places to gather in Simple Community.

While you read this, you are probably within easy distance of a wonderful place to gather that is not currently being used for anything else. There are literally millions of buildings, millions of square feet of indoor space, and millions of acres of land that are great for gathering and not in use this very minute. More than half of the places that are great for gathering are either owned by the public – in other words, owned by you – or by groups of individuals who purchased the space for gathering, but sometimes leave it unused.

There are 8,760 hours in a year.

Wal-Mart Stores are open 100% of those hours, so are hospitals, and hotels, many restaurants, grocery stores and gas stations. Every city is open 24-hours-a-day. These places are always open because they are needed all the time (like hospitals,) because as businesses they can make a profit every hour of the day (like Wal-mart) or both – they are needed and profitable (like hotels).

Local, county, state and national parks are open and available generally from sunrise to sunset, or for somewhere around 35-45% of the hours in a year.

Residential colleges and universities are like mini-cities and are open and available 100% of the time from September through April.

How about high schools?

"Our gym is always full. Groups ask if they can use it all the time. We would like to help. But we need it for our students. The gym stays open and is in use twelve hours a day, seven days a week." High school principals and athletic directors are regrettably forced to repeat statements similar to this all the time. Does that mean our high schools are used 100% of the time as well? Hardly.

I am not suggesting high schools should be open all the time. We have to be sensitive to the impact that overusing facilities has on the quality of education. But there is a big gap between current use and over use.

Most rooms in a school building are used throughout the school day. If the day starts with prep work at six in the morning and the majority of students are gone by five, full-capacity use of the school takes up about eleven hours per day. There are roughly 220 school days per year. Doing the math, the average high school is used at full capacity for about 25% of the year. Certain rooms, like the gym, are used more. And there may be some classes in the evening and during the summer. But the point is that schools provide a lot of unused wonderful places for gathering.

There are also thousands of houses of worship in America. Many of these are magnificent facilities with classrooms, playgrounds, even gymnasiums. Others have significant green space where some have built formal sports fields. When I was in junior and senior high school, I was most fortunate to have a group of about 30 friends. Many times in the summer, we would get together in the early evenings to play softball at a church softball field. I don't know that any of us were members or actually attended services at that church. But those softball games are among the very best memories of my youth.

I am thankful that the church allowed us to use the field. We never asked and they never kicked us off. As near as I can tell, we were the only ones who used the field fully or with any regularity for any purpose. I think about how many religious facilities are used one day per week and sit vacant for the other six. What an incredible place for cultivating Simple Community. The beauty of our softball games was that they happened without a purpose or agenda on the part of the church. Here I am, 40 years later, still remembering the games fondly and thinking positively of the church. I could say similar things about all the basketball games I have played in church gyms over the years.

The vast majority of American houses of worship have their activities clustered on a single day of the week. On that day, most are busy for fewer than 10 hours. Even if you tripled the number of hours to 30 per week and assumed full utilization of the resources during that time, the typical house of worship still sits idle for more than 83% of the hours a year.

Parks, schools and houses of worship are all natural places for gathering. In every case, the primary purpose is the gathering of people. In the case of school, we gather for education. In houses of worship, we have religious fellowship. In the case of parks, the primary purpose is gathering for the sake of Simple Community.

Here is the paradigm shift: The people who own or manage all of these places have, by default, a secondary role. They are property managers and community gatherers with responsibility for the very best places of gathering in America. They do not have a responsibility to provide places and encourage Simple Community, but they have the opportunity and privilege to do so if they choose.

Until now, the vast majority of these people never thought of themselves as property managers or community gatherers. They also never considered the possibility of a secondary role for the properties in their charge – let alone the importance of that secondary mission.

If you are a teacher or principal, I know what you are thinking right now. You just don't have the time to add one more thing to your to-do list.

Relax.

Sometimes the beauty of a paradigm shift is that no further action is required to achieve a new result. You just need to see your current actions in a new light. Right now, all over America, high schools are hosting sporting events, musical programs, art shows, life learning classes and more. However most of these programs are being run from the perspective of the old paradigm. The purpose is primarily for the intentional education of the students.

Teachers and principals encourage people to come to events to support their students. But coaches, music teachers and art teachers have to work very hard just to get parents to attend the events. To entice adults who are not related to the students to come to an event seems near impossible, because they don't think of the events as being of value to the audience.

Here is where the new paradigm starts to come in. If you recognize the need we all have to be more involved with our neighbors, you can recast the value of attendance, transforming it from a task the audience does only to support students into a desirable connection those in attendance share with the students and their neighbors. In other words, invite the neighbors of your place to come to your activities because it is good for THEM too.

Maybe you think you are already doing that. Almost everyone lives relatively close to a neighborhood high school. Even though there is one nearby, there are generally only four times a person is likely to be found on high school property. They are: when the person is a student, when the person has a reunion, when the person has a child in the school, or if the person works at the school. In other words, the high school is not seen as part of the neighborhood. It is seen for the old paradigm value of directly and intentionally teaching high school students.

As close as it is geographically, and as much as school staff might want to think the neighbors are welcomed, very little is actually done to put out the welcome mat to neighbors. Here is an illustration from college.

While I was developing a community engagement strategy for NCAA Division II schools I visited a number of campuses and had a lot of discussions with people touched by the schools in various ways. One meeting at a school included sports boosters, the athletic director, a few coaches and some student athletes. One of the boosters had been the president of the boosters club. He graduated from the school and had stayed and worked in the community of the school. He was also one of the biggest financial supporters of the school.

In this meeting, I asked everyone what they thought it would take to get the neighbors more involved. As part of that line of questioning, I asked the boosters what would make them feel more welcomed. The gentleman I just described said he had often thought he would like to come and walk on the track for exercise but thought it probably wasn't allowed. The athletic director was quick to say that, of course it was fine for him to walk on the track. As I said before though – perception is reality. It wasn't okay, because he didn't feel it was okay. If this man who was so involved and so supportive of the school felt he could not walk on the track, imagine how all the other neighbors of the school felt. They were not directly or intentionally excluded. But they were not invited either.

It takes very little to make your neighbors feel welcomed. You do not have to add any programs to accomplish it. All you really have to do is to think in the light of the new paradigm. Take on a secondary role as the neighborhood gatherer. Define your location as a place where neighbors can gather and let your neighbors know.

All it takes is three touches to make friends. Let me explain through an experience you have probably had and then give some direct tips for how to make that happen at your place. You probably have social activities or events you participate in somewhat frequently. If you do, it probably took only three experiences to determine the experience would be a priority. Different dynamics tend to be at work during each of your first three visits to any social event. The first visit, you take it in and decide if you like it or not. If you like it the first time, you come back again. On the second visit, you become familiar. You discover parts of the experience that may happen every time and others that maybe happen only once in a while. But after two visits, you have a degree of confidence, you know what to expect – enough so, that the third time you may bring a friend. On the third visit, the consistencies of the experience are confirmed. In addition, by the third time you will likely encounter people you saw at both the first two events and you are likely to talk to at least one of them. If you talk to the people, you feel like you belong, and you are likely to make attending this particular activity a priority. If you brought a friend, you share the event with her as if you were an insider because you have a sense of what to expect. It gives you a sense of belonging.

How do you make that happen at your place? Right now, your activities are probably focused on the member participants – the insiders, not on visitors. The goal is to have the secondary purpose of your place be a welcomed destination for your neighbors. Here are three very simple steps to accomplish this goal.

1. **ACKNOWLEDGE YOUR NEIGHBORS:** Whatever the event, put out the welcome mat. Tell them you are happy they are here. Tell them you want to do more to make those who live close to your place to feel more welcomed and that you want them to feel like they are part of the community.

2. **OFFER ALTERNATIVES:** Few do this well at all. If your school is having a basketball game, at half time do an announcement about an activity coming up in the next week other than sports. You want your neighbors to see the diversity of activities. A community is a broad range of things, not just sporting events or plays.

3. **CHANGE YOUR SIGNS:** Most signs on places of gathering are designed for those who already know where everything is. Please test this statement

for yourself. Next time you are on a campus or some other place of gathering where you are not a member, look for signs designed just for the purpose of making you feel welcomed and helping you find your way around. If the signs make it easy for a stranger to join you, more will.

The value of welcoming people should be obvious. Even to the most socially confident people, it just feels better to be sure you are wanted. Offering alternatives might not seem so obvious. Assume for the moment that some people who attend an event do so out of obligation not desire. For example, parents of a musician go to a concert at the school. At that concert they announce an art fair the coming weekend. The parents like art and decide to go, even though their child is not in the fair. Going to the art fair becomes an activity for the parent's benefit, not something they are doing just to support their own child. Something wonderful happens as a result. Another child who is exhibiting in the art fair has his work appreciated by someone who didn't need to be there. I am sure I don't need to elaborate on the value of that.

It really takes very little to engage the community more. You don't need to start new programs; only a change in perspective is required with a more focused message to the benefit of your neighbors.

I don't want to let the neighbors off the hook here. It is not only those who manage places who need to adjust their view. We, who use places, need an adjustment too. There are over 500,000 parks, 25,000 high schools, and 15,000 colleges and universities in America. Most Americans have easy access to one or more of these places. We don't have to ask permission of anyone to take a walk in the park. We are rarely asked to leave if we shoot baskets at an outdoor court at a school. We may even attend an occasional program at a school. However, having easy access to places to gather does not by itself cause Simple Community to happen. Someone has to make it happen. We take for granted the places for gathering, the people who make it happen and the activities that happen there. Rather than seeing the place of gathering as a vibrant site of enriched community, we see an impersonal place where discrete activities happen.

The local parks and recreation department exists specifically to enable Simple Community. One person can start a softball league as long as she has access to a softball field. No field, no league. If you are forming a league, just pick up a phone to organize timing, parks, schedules and the rest. In general, 149 of 150 people playing in a softball league can, and do, take for granted that they can play in a softball league if they want to. They assume that somebody will organize it, that there are parks to play on, and that there will be other people.

In order to use places, the intended use of the space relative to the opportunity for using it for your purposes has to be taken into account. For example, a softball field is always intended for playing softball, but we cannot assume we have the same permission to use a field located at a high school as one at a local park or on a college campus.

In both school illustrations, the primary use of the field is to support education. The field is there to enhance teaching, not Simple Community. One school may have strict policies about using its facilities based on its philosophy of teaching. Focus and concentration on learning may be so important that they have decided not to allow any outside influences or distractions. Another school may have the opposite philosophy, believing that an essential part of learning is to involve people from the community in virtually everything they do.

If you have a larger vision for Building Simple Community you may be tempted to start by building the place, but larger places already exist. In most cases they were neither designed nor intended to cultivate Simple Community. For example, high schools and colleges are designed with education in mind. Houses of worship are for religion. Simple Community can happen in these places too, just not as the highest priority.

Other places, like parks, were intended to be used for community. Roughly one third of adults go to a park every week. That translates into a lot of Simple Community and even greater opportunity. What the parks need are more people, resources, traditions, and stories to make the most of them. At this point, very few places suitable for building Simple Community at the big-picture level are being fully utilized and activities in those places are not nearly as rich as they could be if all the ingredients were in present.

We can't take places for granted. We also can't always expect those who have the fields will also provide the resources to make our softball leagues happen. By December, 2008, it was clear that one impact of the economic crisis would be the reduction or complete elimination of support for parks programs by cities starting 2009 with considerably less tax revenue than they had to support programs in 2008. The full impact of these cuts will not be felt until after Simple Community has been published. Until the economy improves, I suspect in many cases parks and ball fields will still be available but we will be on our own to organize play. I also believe though, that these cuts, while painful in the short term, may be very helpful in the longer term. Hopefully we will not take places and resources for granted after suffering a significant amount of time without them.

CHAPTER 9

How Places are
Preparing for Support

At heart, Simple Community happens in small gatherings, not at huge events. However there are at least two major ways large organizations can – because of their size – dramatically improve the opportunities for Simple Community to take place in small settings. The first is the ability to serve as a clearing house of great ideas that can work at any of their affiliated locations. The second is the ability to identify specific activities that are happening in many different places so they can be supported by corporations and foundations related to the specific activities. I have developed strategies at the college and high school level to accomplish these two goals. In this chapter I will briefly explain the value of the two goals and then explain how it works with colleges through the National Collegiate Athletic Association's Division II (NCAA DII) Community Engagement Strategy and with high schools through the National Federation of State High School Association's (NFHS) Facilitating Community.

Finding the best ideas: Among the many advantages of having associations or federations of schools is the ability to serve as a gathering point for great ideas. All members of the NCAA or NFHS share core common values and a single mission statement. Because of this shared base, most programs or activities that support the efforts of one school may apply to many or all of the rest of the schools in the organization. Both the NCAA DII and NFHS have committed to a focus on supporting community in the way I described as the secondary role of property manager and community gatherer. The NCAA DII has already created a website to support this effort, on which the individual schools can share activities they are doing with their neighbors along with tips for how to do the activity. NFHS is earlier in the process and is exploring doing the same.

Building scale: Over time, these websites will identify particularly distinctive and successful programs that are being duplicated by hundreds or thousands of schools. When that happens, the organization can identify companies or foundations whose products or services could enhance the experience or make it possible for even more schools to participate. The earlier chapter on Remarkable Experiences explained how brands can build real relationships with people by being involved in this very way.

The next chapter lays the foundation for how people, places, and companies can work together to build Simple Community. The remainder of this chapter discusses the development of strategies for NCAA DII and NFHS and how those strategies have put us into a position to realize scalable grassroots programs.

The NCAA Division II Community Engagement Strategy

Colleges and universities are financially supported communities that exist, first and foremost, to educate. However, because of their educational mission, they make a vast array of activities available: classes, sports, music, art, politics, religion, social gathering, and much more. Many even look like a town square. Campuses generally have all the facilities needed to accommodate Simple Community: concert halls, music rooms, art rooms, theaters, every kind of sports platform, and the technological infrastructure that goes along with it.

Colleges have always been dedicated to community service, but community service is not at the heart of Simple Community. The mentality around it is more similar to work or education than how we think about things we do in our spare time. Involvement in community service is beneficial in many ways: it prepares students to be productive members of society; it can give service workers a preview of their chosen disciplines; and it provides an opportunity to give back to the community. But community service is nearly always an agenda of the school, not the community, which means that it is based on the school's programs and goals. They rarely start by meeting with the local neighbors to determine needs and then create community services to match. Even if they did, it would still be service, not Simple Community.

A relatively small shift in focus is already beginning that will fully enable college campuses to become places for Simple Community. Many colleges already make Simple Community opportunities available on campus, but primarily for the college family: students and their families, faculty, staff, recruits & alumni. Less attention and investment has been made to connect with the literal neighborhoods around them.

In 2005, I was invited to make a presentation on Simple Community to a large group of Presidents and Chancellors from NCAA Division II (DII) schools. I talked about the natural opportunity for colleges to be the town square in a service-based economy. I presented ideas for how to bring a better focus to the community surrounding the school – the literal neighborhood surrounding them. In 2006, DII committed to building a community engagement strategy. Over the course of 18 months, I worked with a broad based group of DII school representatives to craft the strategy.

The team developing the DII community engagement strategy came to realize that all we really had to do was a better job of communicating opportunities and coordinating with people on and off campus so that everyone could more easily take part.

The communication and coordination problems are not limited to people without direct connections to the college. To illustrate, I was talking to a group of student-athletes from a variety of sports at a DII school. We talked about community service and Simple Community activities. I asked one student whether her team did either. She talked at some length about several community service programs that her team participated in on a regular basis. Then I asked her what the men's basketball team did. She didn't have a clue. I went around the room. Everyone could talk about their own team's involvement but not anyone else's. It got more interesting from there. I asked the whole group what the music department offers on campus in terms of concerts. I got nothing, not one response. There was little or no communication or coordination of activities between groups. This was found repeatedly on the campuses we visited.

Imagine what would happen on these campuses if the various programs communicated with each other. What if, at halftime of the basketball game, there were announcements about future concerts. They would extend invitations to be a part of the campus community and would make the music students feel appreciated and supported by the athletic department. The basketball team could also invite the art department to exhibit relevant work at their games. The artists would feel valued and appreciated and the basketball team might get some new fans. The benefits of interaction among different departments have wide reaching implications.

Have you ever noticed how many college campuses are built away from the center of town "off on the hill?" They often appear more like fortresses than like communities. The buildings on the outer part of the campus have bare walls facing the community and windows facing the core of the campus. The campus has a beautiful and inviting green with walkways, but it is in the middle of all the buildings where only insiders tend to walk. The intentional purpose of college is to prepare young adults who are living away from home for the first time. The design of most campuses sought to protect the students' safety for the peace of mind of their parents and to avoid the distractions of everyday life so students could focus on their studies.

The protective seclusion of colleges that do not actively seek to build Simple Community with local neighbors often seems uninviting although it may be unintentional. Even if there are no signs prohibiting people from being on campus, there may not be a sense of welcome either. There is no visitor's center, no announcements of events open to the public. There isn't a newsletter distributed to neighbors, or part of a newspaper, a webpage or any other resource that provides a schedule of events and activities open to the public. The neighborhood wouldn't have a good sense for how the school thinks or feels about neighbors or community involvement with the college. There has never been a meeting between the neighbors and the college to talk about what they could do together. The leaders of the college are not actively involved in the programs of the community.

Colleges actively and intentionally engaged with their neighbors look quite different from the rest. Here is an example of what such a college might be like. People living within three miles of the campus tell the same story of how the college has reached out and welcomed them to be more a part of their campus community. Communication about the opportunities open to the neighbors may be found in several places, not the least of which is a weekly section in the local paper. After hearing the college's welcome, one neighbor decided to go to the ice cream social on the campus square to try it out. The jazz band was playing. There was an announcement about a free concert the next Friday. The neighbor came back and brought a friend. During intermission they announced a half-dozen other things neighbors could do including the very popular film series. The neighbor knew nothing of the film series, but from that time on attended every month.

That fall for the first time the neighbor attended a football game and found himself rooting for the team as if it was really his own team. He felt a part of the school, part of the community. When it came time for his sister's kid to go to college, the neighbor's recommendation was powerful because of the bond he had with the school. Prior to the school taking a Simple Community approach with the neighborhood, this neighbor hadn't set foot on campus – though he had lived within a mile of it for over 20 years.

NCAA Division II schools aspire to foster that kind of Simple Community. At the heart of the strategic tools available for the DII community engagement strategy is a website – www.diicommunity.org – of resources designed to support DII schools who want to be more open and supportive of Simple Community as a context. On the website, member schools have the opportunity to share insights on what is working and what isn't. In particular, there is a section called "Ideas that work" where schools can post contexts that have worked for them and offer suggestions to modify or make others better.

The DII strategy group had conservative hopes for the success of the utilization of the website which was designed for the internal use of DII faculty, staff and students directly working on Simple Community. The website has not been broadly publicized beyond those functionally involved in building DII community. There are about 300 schools in Division II. If each school used the website three times a month that would be 1,000 uses a month. Twenty months into the program 20,000 visits would have been a tremendous success. Similarly, we started with 50 ideas that worked. A conservative success in added ideas would have totaled 100 after 20 months.

In less than 20 months online there were over 225 posted ideas and more than 350,000 visits.

I encourage you to browse around www.diicommunty.org. In addition to the hundreds of ideas for drawing community, there are sections on: how to work with others on campus; how to reach out to the community; the role of leadership at the college; research or fact-finding you might consider before creating programs and more.

How NCAA rules speak to the commitment to Simple Community

Probably the least enjoyable role the NCAA plays is rules development and enforcement. The need is clear. In the zeal to gain an edge to win some will bend or break the rules to get better student-athletes on their team. Most new NCAA rules are designed to tighten restrictions after schools have found ways around the rules.

A powerful indication of the NCAA's commitment to building Simple Community in Division II schools can be seen in sweeping legislation that was passed in 2007 which allows student-athletes and coaches to engage in community activities the same as any other member of the college family. This is powerful evidence because the vast majority of NCAA legislation is designed to limit access to high school students for the sake of fairness to competition in recruiting. This sweeping legislation is an act of faith, demonstrating that the schools of Division II value the ability to be engaged as community more than they value finding unfair competitive advantages over one another. It's working. There have been no major violations in over two years since the revisions were passed. More important each year Division II has passed fewer new regulations imposing other restrictions. It seems quite clear the spirit of community is positively influencing the overall environment for sports as well.

The NCAA Division II program is proof that major organizations can be mobilized to contribute their places for building Simple Community. And DII is just getting started. If you have an idea for Simple Community that fits a college campus, call the college closest to you and see if they have a focus on community engagement. Share this book with them. Any effort you invest in bringing Simple Community to a campus will be far easier than if you tried to create the resource yourself.

A reminder – colleges are about education first. Don't make the mistake of thinking they don't care if they say no to some of your ideas. The use of facilities starts with their educational goals. Be prepared to fit in to what they have available. It will still be a step in the right direction.

Putting community back in high school
National Federation of State High School Associations (NFHS)

There are over 25,000 high schools in America[8]. They do not provide the complete community package that college campuses represent. The students don't live at the school. High schools have some of the same resources, but not all. However there are strengths that high schools have as a place which colleges do not. They are bite-sized pieces, schools average fewer than 700 students each – not the 50,000 students found in major universities[9]. This comparatively intimate size makes for a greater likelihood of building a Simple Community idea that can be enjoyed by most or all the people associated with the school. High schools are also largely geographically defined. College students come from all over the country. High School students live near the school.

Perhaps most importantly, high school students are on the launching pad of adulthood. Two-thirds of high school graduates do not go to college. High school is the last shot at preparing them for adulthood – and community life – before they go it on their own. Anyone building Simple Community experiences within the high school context is twice benefited, first by the ease of having a ready place, and second, because of the engaged education you are providing kids on the launching pad.

Fortunately, the National Federation of State High School Associations (NFHS) is a national organization ideally suited to build Simple Community at the high school level. In 2009, they committed to do just that. The approved strategy is called "Facilitating Community." The needs and remedies of Facilitating Community are presented below.

Over the past two decades, the American social landscape has changed in a way that makes the very activities supported by NFHS key to the future success of America's next generation of citizens. The opportunities Americans have to easily gather for the enjoyment of each other have gradually been reduced as the context of work life has migrated from farming (where we worked together as families) to manufacturing (as neighbors) and now to service. Service workers rarely work with the same people for very long and they often work remotely and alone. Farming and manufacturing jobs were passed on from one generation to the next as a way of life, not just a job. Families and neighbors were geographically closer to each other. Work time extended into fun time more naturally. Today, with 80% of Americans working in the highly mobile service sector, most of us need an easier way to reconnect with our neighbors.

While the high school building can be a central social gathering point for a sizable neighborhood, it rarely is. Today, the vast majority of Americans set foot in a high school for only one of four reasons: they are students, they are the parent of a student, they are attending their class reunion, or they work at the school. As a result, adults who do not have children in school – particularly attending high school – may be less inclined to support the school and the co-curricular activities that are vital to social development. The high school has many appropriate facilities and scheduled activities that people would look for in community, but needs support to promote those opportunities to the community. The NFHS and its membership have the opportunity and several good reasons to help high schools become more involved in their communities.

■ *High School students need more quality time with adults other than teachers and parents*

As adults, students will need the confidence and competence to live and work with other adults. In the current service-based economy, high school students lack consistent opportunities to work, play and learn from adults who are neither family nor teachers. Adults don't come to them at the high school and teens are not engaged in the work of their parents. Increasingly more of the communication flow that does take place is impersonal – through the Internet or from inanimate objects.

■ *Americans need more and easier opportunities to gather in enjoyable community settings*

A service-based economy rarely provides the time, places, and resources for most Americans to extend the work environment that was once found in farming and manufacturing economies.

■ *Americans need the relief of community and a greater sense of belonging, now*

America is in the worst economic distress since the Great Depression. High school sporting events and other activities naturally provide simple – and inexpensive or free – ways for neighbors to gather and support each other. Their community can provide needed relief. We seek the comfort of companionship found in deeply rooted but simple community.

High School as Community Solution

American high schools already have the facilities and provide the activities and programs that would promote both the community bonding and the opportunities for students to be meaningfully engaged with unrelated adults. If the high school can be the community gathering place, high school sporting events offer more opportunities for the community to gather than any other. For many younger children, if not most, the first exposure to the high school is an athletic event. High School sports are the natural welcome mat. Other co-curricular activities supported by NFHS – like music, drama and debate – round out the variety of offerings needed to attract a wide and diverse range of community neighbors to be more involved with the high school as a part of their community.

Welcoming unrelated adults to school on a regular basis has several benefits. Not only does it create opportunities for students to learn interaction with adults, it also fosters ideas for how high school students can do more in the community through jobs and volunteerism. It also increases the awareness, understanding and support of the broader needs of the high school experience for adults who might not otherwise consider the importance because they do not have children in school. Compared to past decades, more adults who are eligible to vote on school funding do not have children in school. Involving them in school activities increases the likelihood that they will support sports and other co-curricular activities when it comes time to vote.

What can the NFHS and its members do to support the role of high school in community through this strategy? Realize, first, the needs are real and the best of community has already been created...

"Somewhere in America today..."

- ...a high school team and their community prepare to participate in their first state championship

- ...the senior class is hosting a swing band era dance for the senior citizens in the community

- ...a junior is afraid to ask the owner of the local store for a summer job

- ...ninth graders are planting tomatoes in the urban high school community green garden

- ...families are baking cookies to sell at a high school game tonight

- ...the mayor is participating in a debate with the high school debate team

- ...a dozen of the altos in the high school community choir are parents

- ...the high school orchestra is trying to figure out how to replace a broken timpani drum
- ...a high school student will be a starter in the game for the first time
- ...they are having their 25th annual high school chili cook-off
- ...a woman who graduated in 1960 is wondering what the dress code is in high school
- ...a guy who graduated 10 years ago is building the sets for the high school musical
- ...a high school student will score the game winner she will never forget
- ...over 250 adults who do not have kids in school will come to the art fair at the high school
- ...a sophomore is with a neighbor in the high school auto shop working on a small gas engine
- ...the high school students in the chess club are beating all the adults
- ...the mother of an art student talks to the principal at the school's first art fair
- ...a third-grader will watch a high school sporting event and dream of playing on the team
- ...a high school student is teaching neighborhood adults how to set the clock on a VCR
- ...a retired couple smiles and thinks of the high school musical they attended the night before as they vote for the additional funding for high school activities

NFHS and its membership will not build community. It will reinvigorate and promote community by making known all the wonderful opportunities to be involved with the local high school. The best of community exists in pockets all over America. The best of the best experiences are happening at high schools.

Facilitating Community is a strategy to:

- Identify the most promising activities
- Extend opportunities to others to participate in those activities

- Communicate the opportunities to participate to students and neighbors

- Provide resources to extend the activities most effective at enriching community

- Promote the educational value of high school sports and activities

Simple Community Starters:

- **TALK IT OUT:** Talk with the kids first. Discuss what sparked your interest in building Simple Community. Ask them how they would feel about opportunities to be involved in activities with adults from your town or city. Ask them for suggestions. Then have a similar conversation with a group of teachers. Be sure to be sensitive to leadership issues as mentioned in the DII section. Then get together with the PTA or school administration and a group of kids and teachers to see what might be possible.

- **THINK SIMPLE FUN:** Think water balloon fight. Hopefully, one of the kids will come up with an idea. I suspect it will be harder to get kids involved than adults. I hope to be surprised, but I don't anticipate many high school readers.

- **WHO CARES?** What would make an adult – who doesn't have a kid in high school – want to ever set foot in a high school again? What would make it compelling even for an afternoon or evening?

- **THE MAZE:** During the summer, for one week, the school is converted into an internal corn maze with interesting stops along the way.

- **HAUNTED SCHOOL:** Created by the students at Halloween, a trip through the scariest parts of high school

- **PROFESSOR-STUDENT:** Evening or weekend one-session classes for adults taught by students, on any and everything from their perspective – particularly technology.

- **TRADITIONS:** Look at the thriving traditions at your school and consider reviving pieces that were there when you were a kid

- **HOMECOMING** – is there still a parade?

- **THE MUSICAL**

- **JUNIOR AND SENIOR PROM**

CHAPTER 10
Scalable
Grassroots

Because organizations like the NCAA and NFHS have adopted and are activating strategies to be more involved with their communities, for the first time, there is a way to achieve scalable grassroots and marketing programs in America that benefit communities at the same time.

I began Building Simple Community by defining grassroots marketing – company investments in personalized activity programs in small settings. I went on to suggest that many, if not most, major American companies would invest considerably more in grassroots marketing if they could realize "scale" – the ability to support hundreds, even thousands, of these activities without having to manage them individually.

Later I suggested we needed a new paradigm in marketing that focused on people and their stories as enabled by brands. Partnering with gathering places to provide brand-related resources for Simple Community is the key to achieving scalable grassroots programs. I presented a second paradigm shift for those who manage places of gathering, calling on them to consciously focus on enabling a greater connection with their neighbors. I wrote Building Simple Community to provide guidelines that would enable Americans who enjoy bringing families, friends and neighbors together, to work with marketing professionals who invest in grassroots marketing, and leaders who manage places where we gather naturally.

The work begins here. There are no step-by-step instructions for how to convert ideas about Simple Community into actions. The more I searched for "The five steps towards…" or "Three keys to unlock…" the more I realized that formulas work directly against real, vibrant, Simple Community. The whole point of scalable grassroots is to make each program special and specific to the community where it is taking place. Scalable grassroots works because of a seeming contradiction. It can only work if small places – like individual schools, parks, or places of worship – engage in activities they individually value and manage. But it also only works for those who would invest in those activities if many places do that activity. Among the greater fruits of the NCAA and NFHS strategies will be the ability to identify the many schools, from among the thousands, who independently choose to participate. The organizations will facilitate the support from the brands to those individual schools choosing opt in.

While we were building the strategy for the NCAA Division II schools, people on the advisory board were already coming up with good ideas for their schools. Before the strategy was launched, good programs were already spreading. The ideas in Building Simple Community are still new enough that there are no certainties. I mentioned that my case for Simple Community relies on research and facts. I wrote the book because I had seen enough evidence that when people follow their passion to build community, it happens. So, perhaps, the first constant in successful programs is the person with a passion to see the program proceed. The wonderful development is that now those passionate people do not have to work alone. Using Building Simple Community as a rallying point, the people who bring neighborhoods together, who have places to gather, and who have the necessary resources can work together.

For the first time, the leadership of two organizations, the NCAA Division II at the college level and NFHS at the high school level, are aligned in their thinking about Simple Community and they are encouraging their member institutions to think the same way.

For the first time, there are uniform mechanisms to communicate successful ideas to hundreds and thousands of people able to provide the places to gather and the resources we need.

It is now possible for a company to contact either NFHS or the NCAA and engage in a new kind of meeting on how to work together.

Starting in 2009, these and other organizations will be piloting programs to extend Simple Community. While there is no secret sauce, there is an increasing foundation on which to build. I have also created a website www.mysimplecommunity.com to support the effort.

Here are some components to scalable grassroots. They are not in any order. Investing effort in any of these components can spark enthusiasm and involvement, and the others can be tied in as they make sense.

- "Somewhere in America today…" is a very simple concept, and is intended to be an ongoing reminder that Simple Community is already happening all over America. With the help of the right people, it can flourish and multiply to a point where most, if not all, Americans can access it. Spreading the word about what is already happening is all we have to do to start it. A simple success story can encourage someone to repeat the idea. We do not have to invent new things or think of new ideas. We can build on and copy the wonderful things that are already happening to make opportunities available to more people.

  I got off the train at a different stop last night. It meant walking a few blocks further on a very cold December night, but it also meant walking through four inches of snow in a park in Chicago with a great sledding hill. It was dark out. There were parents with their kids, and teens with small snow boards. There was laughter. I walked – even farther out of my way – through the park on the path made by a sled being taken to the hill. Somewhere in America, people were laughing and riding sleds down a hill in the middle of one of our biggest cities, during the worst financial crisis since the Great Depression. That is the kind of thing we need more of.

- The most immediately promising component of building Simple Community is sharing ideas that already have worked. The NCAA already has this capability on the DII community website. It is like "Somewhere in America today…" but more substantial because there are concise tips written by the people who conducted the activities. They provide insight on the keys to the success and advice for future programs. As the NCAA and NFHS programs mature, you will see more schools try the ideas that work – reaching out to their communities. Each time it will get better, as second, third, and fourth schools try existing ideas and add suggestions for modifications and improvements.

- The best ideas that are posted will be activated more and more often. Once the NCAA or NFHS sees the potential for one idea to be widely adopted by dozens or hundreds of schools, they will be able to approach companies whose products or services may fit with the activity and suggest ways in which the company can participate in extending the activity to even more communities and with even greater resources.

- While Simple Community can thrive entirely on the extension of existing ideas that work, the concept of Remarkable Experiences will be developed to create new ideas and revitalize others, like the revitalization of the high school homecoming parade. Perhaps it is possible to create a Remarkable Experience around the process of building floats. It does not take much imagination to picture an auto manufacturer enhancing the experience by assuring that every float in America is pulled by one of their trucks. The truck, on its own, may not be Remarkable, but having employees of the local car dealership helping to build the winning float of the parade may be.

Now, imagine we have gotten advice from ten different schools that have been holding successful parades for decades and, in every case, there are three things that EVERY school does to organize the parade. In all likelihood, schools holding parades for the first time will have greater success if they do those three things too. Suppose that, because of their success, they have a parade again the following year. Furthermore, the word spreads that there are three key ideas that help to hold a successful parade and more schools jump on the bandwagon – successful parades could proliferate across America!

Before long, parks, places of worship, minor league sports teams, movie theaters, and shopping malls can all have ways to uniformly host uniquely tailored ideas that work. All it takes is agreement on a few simple components and one central organization that is able coordinate the process.

Once we identify the aspects of an experience that can be modified depending on the context, we can identify how products or brands can help to support those aspects. In the same way that we identified a need for floats to be pulled by pickup trucks, a company could agree to provide a relevant and useful resource for any school that follows the three key ideas of any event.

The beauty of this approach is that it relies on activities that are already being done successfully, provides a way for the brand to be meaningfully connected to the idea, and allows for scale. A company can test the idea in just a few places with low cost and risk, and, by collaborating with parent organizations such as NCAA or NFHS, it can extend successful programs far more easily.

Over the past five years, the work of organizations like NFHS and the NCAA have paved the way for building Simple Community with grassroots programs. I believe the blueprint to completing the task is to be found in the hearts of those who crave a stronger community, and in the passion of leaders and marketers who recognize that America is at a time of unique need, when investing in building Simple Community makes sense.

Earlier this year, I met with a company considering investing millions of dollars per year in the infrastructure needed to facilitate the creation of the high school community and the website, which will serve as the gathering point for suggestions and ideas that work at the high school level. There were several business units in the room and certainly a considerable amount of doubt about how building the Simple Community initiative would make money. The discussion got a bit sidetracked as separate business units were trying to frame the opportunity in the way most favorable to them. The discussion got animated and it became evident that people were passionate about the idea. However, the nagging question of why the company should invest deeply to help build community when there was no proven approach for success, was throwing a serious wrench in our progress. Finally, the top executive ended the discussion with a single, seemingly indisputable statement: "Because it's the right thing to do." And so it is.

How many of America's greatest companies were started by people risking failure because of their vision of success? Many of those leaders suffered bankruptcy and other forms of personal or corporate ruin along the way, but they persisted because they knew that the time was right, the components were in place, and the need was there. Whether they did it out of the good of their hearts or to become rich beyond measure, with the right people working together and determined not to fail, they achieved their vision.

We have it all with Simple Community. The time is right, millions of people have expressed their passion and are motivated to help, and a minimal investment by companies will make a huge difference in America at a time of extreme need. This service-based economy will never bring people together or build community. It is the right thing to do and we have to take it upon ourselves.

CHAPTER 11

A Call to Action

There are at least five ways brands can benefit by investing in Simple Community.

1. **BRING BRAND-RELEVANT RESOURCES TO COMMUNITIES:** People know enough about products and services. They have more than enough choices. People need and want more fulfilling time together. Think about how your brand fits in Simple Community and invest in experiences that will lead to stories which naturally include appreciation for what you invested to make the experience possible.

2. **BRING VALUE TO EXPERIENTIAL MARKETING:** During a strategic positioning meeting on redefining experiential marketing I once asked for a definition of the current positioning of live experiences. I'll never forget this, our IT guy said, "It's the mindless execution of things the client really doesn't want to do." Stop mindless executions of live experiences that have the ROI equivalent to hauling dirt in a limo, and replace it with a new measure of value: the story.

3. **BRING SCALE TO GRASSROOTS:** Have you noticed how many American companies have gone green – gotten conscious – about environmental concerns? An internal voice is telling them to do more than just sell things; they need to provide real

solutions for real problems. Companies have been choosing to go green instead of supporting communities because they can change light bulbs and control environmental outputs, but they cannot build Simple Community without a context. We cannot expect companies to build those contexts, but if there were a method they could take advantage of, which brought passionate people together with the places and organizations designed for gathering, companies would invest in communities. Make scalable grassroots marketing a reality. Be open to discussions with the other two groups. Start the discussions yourself. I have talked to at least a dozen experiential marketing brand side executives who, to this point, have not been able to get the attention of senior management to invest in grassroots. I hope the spread of Simple Community will give you the ammunition you need.

4. **TURN DOWN THE ALARMS OF ADVERTISING:** $300 billion is too much. If just ten percent of that were invested in Intentional Remarkable Experiences, providing resources to communities, we would have a changed nation. At the end of the day I don't go home to experience more, faster, bigger. I want relaxation and enjoyment, just like everyone else. IREs offer a new way to meaningfully interact with people who will consequently thank and welcome you instead of zapping you with their alarm defenses.

5. ACT ON THE NEW MARKETING PARADIGM.

Think People. Not consumers.

What do you call the PEOPLE who buy your products or services? Do you ever, under any circumstances, think of yourself as anything but an individual? Have you ever introduced yourself, "Hi, I'm a potato chip eater?" Are you a "target," a "demographic," or a "preferred gold user?" I think not. Market research tools have become sophisticated enough to surgically identify people with target traits in the sweet-spot of a core demographic. But the results pinpoint data points, not people. Our sharp focus is through the barrel lens of our rifle, our intent. There are great opportunities for those who start by looking at needs and wants from their point of view. By thinking about the nature of simple gathering and asking how your product or service enhances that, you acquire their view and can see where you really fit.

Spend ninety percent of your budget on targeted messaging strategies. But if you are going to do real things with real people, treat them as people, from their perspective, first. If you invest ten percent of your marketing in IREs that build Simple Community, you will satisfy your business experiential marketing business needs while giving people what they need. Sell to the potato chip eater with ninety percent of your budget, but invest ten percent in the life of a person who also happens to eat potato chips.

Stories. Not messages.

100 million websites. $300 billion dollars. We don't need more information, we need more opportunities. Advertising messages don't bring commitment. Remarkable Experiences do. Stories are the evidence of life. Thoughtful investment in building community will be followed by stories.

Theirs. Not yours.

You might be tempted to that think this shift will be easy. However, you cannot just create a story and get your consumers to tell it. If you do, you will be advertising, not providing opportunities for true Remarkable Experiences. Your stories, no matter how good or creative, are from the old paradigm. IREs only work when PEOPLE create them and retell THEIR stories.

The hardest part in this paradigm shift is giving up control. Advertising in the mass media age controlled messages easily. With enough weight, your message could indeed change the world. Today even $300 billion worth of messages can't do it. Stories work. We miss and long for the simple things in life, and stories shared between individuals about how a brand made it possible for them to hang out with friends are the messages of the future. The ability to manipulate new media with terms like "social networking" and "engaging" doesn't make it so. Have you been hugged by the Internet today? Does a commercial with great scenery make you feel refreshed? It is indeed a brave new world. It's theirs, not yours. You can't have it back, but you can make quite a good living with them in it.

I have a great story from a time that I was hanging out with some neighbors at our local park. I am dying to tell it! I have already told it many times. My friends have all heard it and sometimes they ask me to tell it again – Which I do. Some of my friends have told my story to others. I'd love to tell it to you sometime...

(Endnotes)

1 *The Seven Habits of Highly Effective People:* 15th Anniversary Ed. Stephen R. Covey (2004) Free Press.

2 *Purple Cow: Transform Your Business by Being Remarkable.* Seth Godin (2002) Portfolio/Penguin.

3 The first was a study of high school students in 1984. Since then I have done more than 20 national studies of time use and leisure activity. By far, the most useful resource has been the *ESPN Sports Poll* which I created in 1994. The Sports Poll covers most aspects of free time – sports interests in depth. The study is a nationally representative telephone sample of Americans ages 12+. There is also a kids' version for 6-11 year-olds. Interviews have been conducted 360 days a year since January of 1994 with a total of more than 200,000 completed interviews. In addition, since 1995 I have partnered with Nielsen, ICR and TNS, NPD, and Harris to conduct polls on aspects of American culture that impact free time.

4 Key to the research on the eight buckets is the individual perspective of what an activity fulfills. For example, if a person bikes for exercise, they would consider biking part of sports and exercise. If they bike because they like to be outdoors, they would think of it as outdoor activity. What the person thinks of it as is what it should be. That there is overlap in concepts is covered by the primacy of how it is classified in the mind of the individual.

5 *Commitment-Led Marketing: The Key to Brand Profits is in the Customer's Mind.* Jan Hofmeyer and Butch Rice (2000) John Wiley.

6 *All Marketers Are Liars: The Power of Telling Authentic Stories in a Low-Trust Word (2005)* Seth Godin – Portfolio

7 *Made to Stick: Why Some Ideas Survive and Others Die (2007)* Chip & Dan Heath – Random House

8 25,476 secondary schools based on 2003-04 data from: *Institute of Educational Services, Department of Education, Digest of Education Statistics 2007*, Table 5: *"Number of educational institutions, by level and control of institution: Select years, 1980-81 through 2005-2006."*

9 Institute of Educational Services, Department of Education, Digest of Education Statistics 2007

What people are saying about Simple Community:

"Simple Community delivers a seriously needed message at just the right time. The Living side of the book helps us all understand how we lost community and the Building side shows us how to get it back. In this very short book you are sure to find a handful of new insights that will simply add more joy and value to the time you spend with your family, friends, and neighbors. And if it really grabs you, "Simple Community" will show you ways to do far more for your community than you thought possible before you picked up the book."

Ken Dychtwald, Ph.D., best-selling author of *With Purpose: Going from Success to Significance in Work and Life*

. . . .

"I found Simple Community to be insightful, compelling in its approach and an absolute joy to read. I found myself nodding my head in agreement on many occasions. It outlines a vision for the personal and economic development of our future and points us in a positive direction. If asked what I thought of it I would likely reply — If you are ready for some serious thinking about the future of America, then I suggest you read this book."

Robert Kanaby, Executive Director of the National Federation of State High School Associations (NFHS)

. . . .

"Stories are the proof that life has taken place when people gather. That thought alone from Simple Community makes this book worth reading. Most of the books I write are really story books about the best things that happen between people. Rich has taken the importance of stories to another level. After reading Simple Community you will recognize the power of your life stories to encourage those around you and motivate more of the best of simple community."

Ronda Rich, best-selling author of *What Southern Women Know About Faith*

. . . .

"Simple Community is both easy and challenging to read—easy because so much of it rings true and is written in a personal style; challenging because the insights offered are sobering. Suggestions are practical, realistic and attainable. Rich's book shows that it takes only a little time and effort to benefit by extending community— the payoff quickly outweighs the efforts involved."

Mike Racy, Vice President of Division II, The National Collegiate Athletic Association

"If you are in business, Simple Community will be like LASIK surgery enabling you to more clearly see who to reach and what to do once you are there with them. In essence, Simple Community has defined the intersection between life and consumer marketing. For years, brands have tried to find tangible ways to invest in community and build business. Rich has provided the road map to do just that."

Tim Schoen, Vice President, Sports & Entertainment Marketing, Anheuser-Busch/InBev

....

"Minor League Baseball is all about community. Understanding the role that our clubs play within there respective communities is the cornerstone of any successful club. "Simple Community" provides great insight into why Minor League Baseball has been such an integral part of these locales and goes beyond that to show us how to find the best of community when we are away from the local ball park too."

John Cook, Senior Vice President, Business Operations, Minor League Baseball

....

"Luker makes two seemingly unconnected observations: society is increasingly in need of opportunities for Simple Community. Advertisers are experiencing declining returns from their information campaigns. However Luker makes a strong case that the business sector can help society in its quest for more community and reap the benefits for their product at the same time. Luker's 25 years in research, coupled with a deep sense of the human condition, gives him a vantage point to call for a paradigm shift in advertising. This book is a must read for citizens and advertisers alike."

Jerome Johnston, Ph.D., Research Professor, University of Michigan and author of *Positive Images: Breaking Stereotypes with Children's Television*

....

"Rich has found a way to enrich the relationship between college and college town at a time when both are finding it harder to make ends meet. His book – and his work – are unusually sensitive to the differing needs of various groups who work and live together in community. Rich's years working with NCAA Division II schools have paid off in Simple Community which is a guide that makes it easier for schools and organizations of all kinds to work together. The approach will lead to more fulfilling community, better education, and more cooperation among us all."

Dr. Charles Ambrose, President, Pfeiffer University and Immediate Past Chair, NCAA Division II Presidents Council -

Richard Luker, Ph.D.

With the publication of Simple Community, Rich is now turning his attention to helping communities, organizations and American companies work together to enrich community life in America. Rich's background leading to Simple Community is covered in the preface to the book. Rich and his wife Vicki live in Fairview, NC and St. Petersburg, FL.

Living
Simple
Community

By
Rich Luker, Ph.D.

Published by Tangeness Press, St. Petersburg, FL
Printed in the United States of America
Library of Congress Control Number: 2009929066
"Simple community" (ISBN 9780615299112)

Acknowledgements

I have an entire community to thank for their thoughts and contributions to this book. Topping the list is Caitlin Bonham who has read it and commented on it at least as many times as I have. If you enjoy the read, you have Caitlin to thank for that.

David Pickle, the managing director of publishing for the NCAA is responsible for introducing my community work to the NCAA in the first place. Beyond that, he kindly took the time to suggest the structure for the book which I ultimately adopted. David introduced me to Arnel Reynon who designed the cover and produced the layout and art for the book. Thanks Arnel.

Several people read various versions and provided helpful advice along the way. Chandra Lim and Sara Whitaker in particular challenged me on several key concepts in the book. Other helpful readers included Dennis Boyle, Leo Fitzpatrick, Alison Jenks, Abby Bennett, and Judy Shoemaker.

I am deeply indebted to the NCAA and NFHS for the opportunity to work with them on creating community engagement strategies. I can't possibly name everyone involved but I need to single out a few in each organization who share my passion for building community and worked tirelessly to make it happen in their organizations.

In the NCAA that would include Division II Vice President Mike Racy, and Director, Terri Steeb. During the development of the strategy Dr. Chuck Ambrose, was the Chairman of the Division II Presidents and Chancellors Council. He served two terms. Chuck was the ideal leader for this strategy. At the same time,

Jill Willson was the head of the Division II Management Council. If there was anyone more supportive (still) of the community initiative than Jill, I don't know who it is. I consider them all friends. I also owe a big debt of gratitude to the members of the committee who worked with me to develop the overall strategy. Dennis Cryder and JoJo Rinebold are long time friends and were steadfast supporters throughout the development of the strategy.

Judy Shoemaker, the head of Marketing for NFHS, has been the champion of community within NFHS. She brought me in to speak to the group initially and has worked side-by-side with me ever since. With her love and commitment to the development of high school students combined with a stellar marketing career, she was the ideal person to assure a high school community strategy would remain honest to the mission of NFHS and provide for needs into the future. That said, the incredible passion for the well-being of students, and the friendship and support of NFHS executive director Robert Kanaby and Robert Gardner, the chief operating officer are both deeply appreciated. Finally, I am honored with the trust of the NFHS Board of Directors and state executives in the support they have shown for the community strategy.

I also want to mention two people I met by chance on separate occasions while flying across America. First, Pat O'Connor had just become President of Minor League Baseball when we met. Thanks to Pat (and John Cook), I have been able to more actively support community initiatives with MiLB.

My second chance encounter was with Susan S. who is a member of a family who owns a noted American company. I was working on the book on the flight and she asked me about it. Her kind words and encouragement went a long way toward developing new, more community-friendly ways of opening doors at major American companies.

I sought advice from many people about how best to distribute the book once it was finished. In particular, I want to thank Ken Dychtwald, who has published more than a dozen books on aging, for his help throughout. Doris Michaels took time from her agency to provide helpful advice on the publishing process as well. My friends C. J. Lonoff, Jan Fermback and Stephanie Reaves were among the earliest to support the idea of writing in the first place and to encourage me when I was having a hard time getting started.

Finally, to my Myrtle Beach buddies, Duane, Lou and Dan, many thanks for being my Simple Community for more than thirty years.

Dedication

This book is dedicated to my wife
and true partner in everything I do,
Vicki, and our children
(Anna, Melissa, Dan and Abby).

Table of Contents

Read this side of the book first if...

- You wonder how technology is impacting community life

- You want to enjoy more time with your family and friends

- You believe more time with family and friends will help us get through these trying times

- You want to pass on strong community relationships to the next generation

Preface

For years I have been speaking to groups about the importance of people gathering with their friends and family. For nearly as long, the audiences have been encouraging me to write a book on the subject.

By studying history and through my own research I have become very passionate about the importance, the need for and the lack of community, Simple Community – playful, enjoyable time with others, without an agenda or work objective. It seems the passion is contagious. The more time passes, the more often I get asked to speak to groups about Simple Community. I wish I could always say yes, but I can't anymore. Besides, I don't think that my presentations alone will do enough to encourage people to live their lives with more Simple Community. This book is my attempt to reach farther with a message that will hopefully encourage people to make the enjoyment of time with others a higher priority in their lives.

I have been studying everyday American life for over 25 years. It started with a growing concern that American teens were struggling with life's purpose and with developing quality relationships. For my doctoral dissertation in graduate school I studied theories of adolescent social development and conducted a series of studies with American teens on the quality of their relationships with parents, individual friends and peer groups. I wondered if American teens turned to TV and other media when they felt distressed. I am happy to say, the research found that the vast majority of American teens have strong nurturing relationships, which provide them with the support they need. The minority of American adolescents who do struggle rarely rely on the media as a source of support or direction.

Despite the overall good news, my research left one enduring question going back to the first study in 1979. We know that relationships produce many benefits including increased health and happiness. So why isn't enjoyment of others a higher priority in American culture today? There are dozens of books about how communities can and should "work" together. They focus on community service – working for the good of others – or community activism – fighting for the rights of others. They advocate empowering communities – how to influence government and commerce to provide needed resources. All are important, serious needs. But I could not find one book on why or how we should play

together as neighbors and communities for the good of all. Play for the good of all – it even sounds frivolous.

I arrived at an understanding of the need for Simple Community by a curious path. It took nearly twenty years to fully grasp it.

For most of my career I have studied the concept of free time and how Americans spend their time when they don't have to work, go to school, or fulfill other obligations. The most telling finding from that research is that most Americans believe they have substantially less free time than they actually do. If you ask people how much free time they have, they usually say little to none. But when you work with them to figure out how they have spent their time recently, they usually discover that they have far more than they realized.

"I am too busy to get together with you." Perception is reality. If we think we have less time, we live that way. We minimize or reduce the amount of time we choose to spend enjoying each other's company. Even though I repeatedly saw in the studies that we feel we have little time, I didn't connect it with our need to prioritize enjoying time with others. I am certainly far more guilty than most of doing serious things at the expense of the truly fulfilling and valuable enjoyment of others. But I didn't realize it until I understood the need for Simple Community.

In the early part of my career, while I taught at Temple University, I studied the role of television in American society and consulted on the creation of television shows that sought to provide a blend of entertainment and educational content. A bad year for baseball on television started me on the path of researching the role of sports that led to my study of community.

When CBS lost hundreds of millions of dollars in one year on their investment to broadcast Major League Baseball (MLB) games, I asked a team of graduate students to find the research that CBS or MLB used to arrive at the financial value of rights to broadcast those games. They found nothing. In 1988 there was not one significant study dedicated to the role of sports in American life. Not one, even though the sports industry generated billions in revenue every year.

In response, I spent years studying sports in general and then approached ESPN in 1993 with a business plan to systematically study sports in America. My work culminated in the creation of the ESPN Sports Poll which was launched in January of 1994. In over 15 years of nearly daily interviewing, over 200,000 Americans have been surveyed on their broad interests and sports activities. Over that time, more than 2,000 different questions have been included to monitor

the overall landscape of sports in America. Through the ESPN Sports Poll I was able to watch the National Football League overtake Major League Baseball as America's favorite sport in 1994 – the year the MLB season ended early because of a strike.

But the Sports Poll became an important measure of the role of sports in America as we studied the connection between sports and how Americans handled hard times. Following 9/11 I was able to provide insight to the sports leagues, media and sponsors on how Americans felt about sports during a crisis. Many sponsors were considering withdrawing from sports sponsorship altogether until it was over. There were discussions of canceling the remainder of sports seasons. But the research told us that we needed the exact opposite. During the worst of times we need relief. During bad times we are comforted by spending and enjoying time with those we love. We know this from the research during the decline of tech stocks at the end of the 1990s and again in a major economic crisis in 2008. During hard times, Americans need relief and they see time with friends and family and the enjoyment of sports as a key source of relief.

It took more to fully understand the need for Simple Community than the realization that sports and other sources of fun provide relief. While I was studying the history of how free time activity and interest in sports in America changed over time since the 1800s, I came to the realization that how we work together, not specifically what we do, seems to be the strongest connection to what we like and turn to as a source of relief. A major section of Simple Community is devoted to America's transition from agriculture to manufacturing to service as the primary source of how we make a living. The service economy no longer provides the time, place and natural contexts for gathering that were common to farming and manufacturing economies.

One final, key piece of the need for Simple Community became clear to me as Internet use took hold in America. Many people seem to think "social networking" through digital media will provide all the community we need. I disagree. Being in the same place at the same time is at the heart of relationships. New technologies provide us with more enhanced ways to communicate when we can't be together, but mediated communication will never replace being there.

Being a technology-driven, service-based economy makes it easier for us to work alone and readily change what we do for a living from time to time. Work is no longer a way of life, it is just a job. I am convinced that our realization that Simple Community, playfulness, and recreation are necessities, not optional

niceties, is way overdue. They provide relief in distressing times. Simple Community re-creates us. It allows us to replenish our energy, recharge the batteries, and remind ourselves that we work as hard as we do for the sake of being in a community with those we love.

With the need more clearly understood, the major breakthrough for developing Simple Community came in 2005 when I was asked by the National Collegiate Athletic Association (NCAA) to address the first large meeting of Division II college presidents and chancellors on the topic of building community on college campuses. I had first talked about colleges as town squares in 2004 because it seemed to me that colleges were the last remaining, financially supported context able to provide Simple Community to a significant group of people. Shortly after my presentation to the NCAA Division II presidents they committed to developing a significant strategy to encourage broader community activity on their campuses and they asked me to lead the effort. I worked on the creation and activation of that strategy with an advisory group comprised of people in key positions in Division II schools for the next 18 months. The key goal was to enable greater connection between students, the campus community and the larger neighborhood of those who live near the school.

Early on we realized that our best resource to enable schools to work together would be the creation of a website to provide tips on how to reach out to the community. An important element of the website was a section providing ideas that worked on individual campuses. Our belief was schools would be most motivated and encouraged by following the successes of other schools. The website was launched in February, 2007. It was intended for the internal use of the roughly 300 schools of Division II and was not publicized outside the regularly distributed information to those schools. I think everyone would have been thrilled if, by the end of 2008, we had 25,000 visitors to the website from people trying to build Simple Community. As I write this preface in January, 2009, there have been over 350,000 visits to the site. Simple Community has taken root in ways we could not have predicted and I am convinced that we are just seeing the beginning of the success and positive impact that Division II schools – and other colleges and universities will experience – as they actively open their doors to the community.

At the beginning of 2008 I started working with the National Federation of State High School Associations (NFHS) on a parallel strategy for high schools titled "Facilitating Community," which was adopted by the Board of Directors in

2009. If college campuses are the town squares, high schools are the neighborhood centers. The work with NFHS has been well received and will produce tremendous opportunities for high schools around America to offer richer experiences for their students. At the same time, the strategy is creating new opportunities for adults in the community who do not have students at the school to become more involved through the broad range of activities offered by the high school.

I did not start my career thinking I would devote my life to building Simple Community. It just turned out that way. From the time I completed my doctoral work I have engaged in academic/scholarly work, maintaining faculty status pretty much throughout the years, currently at Northwestern University. At the same time, I have always believed it is important and valuable to find ways to utilize scholarly learning to improve the quality of life, so I have worked in the commercial sector for most of my post-graduate years. The combination of those experiences is vital to this book. My scholarly work has given me perspective on American social life. My commercial work has allowed me to see the opportunity for the American business community to do more to enable Simple Community in a way that also helps their business. If given the choice between exposure to 1,000 advertisements, or one community experience made possible by a relevant company, which would you choose? Just now, American companies are beginning to realize that there is much to be gained by investing in the real lives of people. Consider, for example, the proliferation of corporate "green" initiatives and advertising campaigns which show sensitivity to the need to protect the environment.

Simple Community is my attempt to tie together 25 years of work and research on the importance of – the need for – greater opportunities for us to gather and enjoy each other. I continue to be surprised that we don't realize this on our own, but, for whatever reason, many, if not most of us, feel guilty about investing in the enjoyment of life. We do not recognize it for the necessity it is. By reading and passing along the thoughts in this book I hope you will be able to embrace, build and find more Simple Community in your life and with those you love.

I have presented most of what you are about to read to audiences dozens of times. At this point, it is almost impossible for me to think about this material as a writer rather than as a speaker. This book is not intended to be a piece of literature. Please read it for the message.

(The preface is the same for Building Simple Community.)

PART ONE:
The Need

Simple Community is

PEOPLE

taking TIME to gather together

in a PLACE suited to enjoying each other.

They bring the RESOURCES needed to have fun.

The best times give rise to STORIES that they tell again

and again. When they are really lucky, something happens

that creates a TRADITION, which begs to be repeated.

These are the six ingredients of Simple Community.

Six Things That Tell Us We Need More of Each Other

e encounter things in our everyday lives that illustrate our need for more of each other. They may be things we read about or personal experiences. It might be something that comes as a result of just thinking about how America is now or how it has changed. Whatever those things are, I do not believe they show up often enough or powerfully enough to get us to do something about it. Before getting into how and why we seem to have less of each other, I want to attempt to spark some thoughts that will make the reality of the need more clear before we tackle what to do about it.

1. Snowstorms tell us we need more of each other. A story:

It was the first time I thought of a car as a social cocoon, and, strangely enough, the awareness came from being outside the car, not in it. A full day had already been lost to a blizzard and people were slowly realizing that they would have to venture outside long before they could use their cars. So there we all were, walking through town in the snow in the middle of a major four-lane street. The only sounds were the wind, the snow crunching under our feet, and the voices of strangers talking to each other: happy, curious strangers. Being without cars and struggling to go a block didn't feel like a hardship. It felt more like being transported back to a time when people walked and talked together regularly. I helped people who were stuck in the snow and felt certain that, if I were stuck, they would have helped me. For a few days, the storm eliminated the influence of the car.

I realized that every day I pass hundreds – thousands – of people in cars. They come within feet of me, but I don't appreciate them as individuals. I can see them through the windows, but the car shelters all my other senses and I am isolated. "Defensive driving"– designed to avoid accidents and save lives – has unintentionally defined others on the road as the enemy. Although cars get me quickly from point A to point B, it is at the expense of a simple, quiet, meaningful connection with the people around me.

An evening thunderstorm that causes a power outage can have the same effect, forcing candlelight and conversation to replace lights and television. I also feel

it on the rare days that I am somewhere without access to the Internet. During these times, when I am left to my own devices to make life interesting, I am much more likely to turn to those around me. Circumstances that I can't control help me to close the desire gap between the amount of time I want to spend with others and the amount of time that I actually do.

2. American buildings tell us we need and want more of each other.

For some years I had a hunch that people change their living environment in response to historical events that make them feel more secure or more at risk. To test that hunch, I explored government statistics of home building and improvement, to identify the trends in home construction over the past 50 years. The progression in building trends from the 1950s to today is really quite interesting, and quite telling.

Often when I speak to groups, I ask them to tell me the strangest feature that Americans added to their homes in the late 1950s and '60s. They tell me waterbeds and skylights. Few ever mention bomb shelters.

Bomb shelters:

During the cold war in the late '50s and early '60s – particularly following the Cuban missile crisis – Americans built cement block rooms in their basements for protection against atomic bombs. Kids at school did drills to practice getting under their desks. Obviously, we didn't know much back then about the completely devastating power of nuclear bombs.

During that same period, America endured several major city riots and frequent anti-war protests. People responded by building ranch style housing with the windows at the top of the walls – harder to break, and harder to get in. Americans in the '60s felt a greater need for safety. New home construction reflected that insecurity; we built bomb shelters and smaller windows – no porches and no decks. Additional fences were also a common order of the day.

The Fleming Building

My favorite illustration of insecurity reflected in construction is the administration building at the University of Michigan, built in the late '60s. There were frequent protests at the university during the

Vietnam War. Students would storm the old administration building and hold sit-ins in the president's office, often protesting through the night. Michigan created a decades-long solution to a period of insecurity that lasted three years. The Fleming building, while artistic enough, has no windows to easily break and on the first floor, no offices – just an elevator.

Few things in the '70s and '80s threatened American security to the extent that the events of the '60s had. The mid 1970s through the 1990s were one of the better times in American history. The Viet Nam war was over. Economic woes driven by an oil crisis in the Middle East had lifted. There were far fewer protests than during the 1960s.

As the country enjoyed greater stability and security, I expected a change in our housing to reflect a greater desire to seek out interaction with others as a reflection of better and safer times. It took until the 1990s to get there, but we did.

Americans came out of their shells more in their building styles. Among the most popular components of new homes and additions in the '80s were decks. They provided living space, out in the open, but at the back of the house. People felt safe enough to be outside with family and friends, but not quite secure enough to be out front with strangers. Still, it was a big step forward from bomb shelters. By the 90s, government records of building trends show an increase in the percentage of homes that included front porches large enough to have seating areas.

Trends in housing weren't the only thing that reflected Americans' fears and their need for security. In the '50s, downtowns were vibrant and active places and the center of shopping. The Sears store, drug stores with soda fountains, and dime stores were downtown along with restaurants and clothing stores. It was the town center, complete with the town square and the movie theater. The shopping mall of the '60s and '70s killed many downtowns.

The real motivation behind the creation of malls is open to debate. Some say it was all about parking. Certainly the creation of more business was a deciding factor. I think it was more about safety. The next time you go to a mall, if you ever do, notice the nature of older malls. They are like fortresses. No exposure to humans from outside the walls. Also, notice that most malls have a security force, something rarely seen in the downtowns of old.

By the 1990s, modifications to American buildings and downtowns really demonstrated the desire for more Simple Community. Mall traffic slowed significantly and gave way to Lifestyle Centers[1] – stores in outdoor format with interspersed play areas. Downtowns became more vibrant again. The big stores

never returned to the downtown area, but restaurants, coffee shops and other social gathering places replaced them. Once again, downtown was becoming a place for community to gather.

So hear the voice of desire for community in the buildings around you. What are your neighbors saying in the openness (or lack thereof) of their homes? Notice the open-space malls. Notice the return of small shops and restaurants to our downtowns. Our buildings show, that even if we don't know it, we are asking for more Simple Community.

3. Picnics and multi-tasking tell us we need more of each other.

If my mom were still alive, she might have a hard time defining the concept of multi-tasking. She died in 1994 having never experienced the Internet. Many more American children alive today have never experienced a picnic. I think those kids are missing out on more than my mother did.

This next story may be a painful read, but the message isn't. It's the pace that may trouble you. You may feel a powerful urge to hit the fast-forward button. But take a breath and stay with me on this.

There was a time, not too long ago, when an American family would get up on a Saturday morning, do a few things around the house, pack a picnic basket, some books, some games, maybe a ball or two and go to the local park. They might get there around ten in the morning. They would spread everything out on a blanket, and... well, maybe just lie around for a while. Then maybe they would read a book. They might throw a ball around, then walk over to the stream and throw some rocks across. They'd run around the bases to see who was the world's fastest, come back to the blanket laughing, hot and sweaty for some lemonade. They'd eat, fend off some ants, and lie around some more. They might play tag, or maybe capture the flag. Someone might pick flowers, while someone else walked around just to think for a while. And by the time they packed up to go home, it was five o'clock. All these things were done one at a time.

No, really, I was actually at picnics like that in the early 1960s when I was a kid. I asked people to read early drafts of this book and a few suggested that I alter this section because it was too idealistic. I sat at the keyboard for the longest time thinking of how to do that when it struck me, "No, it really was just like that."

You survived the story. These days, it is a very hard choice to pass a day with such simplicity. History has proven that, if the family in the story were presented

with the choice or the ability, they would have done more. In 1960 we did not have as many options as we do today. Technology has enabled the explosive development of tools and toys that allow us to do many more things, faster, and often at the same time. Americans are using and adapting to new technology as quickly as it is being presented to them. PRESENTED. These things just showed up one day and we started using them. Now we are doing more, faster, better... I think. Often, we do many things at the same time. But something more than picnics is getting lost in multi-tasking. That picnic, while perhaps painfully slow to consider today, somehow had it all together. It was life. It was the whole thing. Life was about what families, friends, neighbors and communities did. Now we have many parts and pieces. Some are enjoyable, others are necessary, but fitting them into a fulfilling whole is proving to be very challenging.

4. Street lights and kids at play tell us we need more of each other.

A study of children aged 6 – 11 from the 1990s[2] found that the typical 8-year old had less than an hour of unstructured playtime per day. Kids used to play sports – emphasis on play – a different sport every season. They would play pick-up games when they weren't playing in leagues. They would use socks rolled up together as balls and sticks as bats. They would invent their own games or rewrite the rules for the traditional games. They played in each other's yards. They knew the neighborhood – which houses had what fruit trees, the best places to hide for capture the flag. They would play together until dark, often every night of the week. One of the great joys of parenthood was hearing the kids play in the neighborhood. Sometimes kids got hurt. They got cuts, and bumps and bruises, even broken bones. But they played until the streetlights came on.

Current parents reading that may cringe. Who would let their kid play unsupervised in the neighborhood, especially at night? Well, in the '50s and '60s, most parents did. Kids walked to the park alone and played all day without incident. Well... not quite. The fact is the '50s and '60s were much more dangerous for kids playing in parks than post-2000. How is that possible?

Two key factors are at work. First, back then there wasn't enough media capacity to report every bruised knee. I trust I am not alone in being baffled when CNN stops programming for "breaking news" that turns out to be an overturned truck in Georgia. Is that really national news? I guess it is, because there they are with a live feed from the scene. In the past, there were three main resources

to cover the daily news: a local paper, three relatively primitive TV networks and their affiliates, and a few radio stations. These resources were not enough to cover the critical news of the day, much less accidents at the local playground. They cover "bruised knees" today because there are more hours available for news broadcasting than there are stories to fill them. As a natural result, the dangers we perceive in the world get blown out of proportion.

And second, perhaps a positive side to the overkill in reporting is that it has made parents more cautious – the likely real cause of safer parks. Kids rarely play without an adult nearby these days. That's a good thing.

The bad thing is that, because parents need to supervise, the consequence is often less time for play. Sports have become more work and more scheduling than play. Kids specialize these days. They pick a sport, learn it, practice it – work at it really – all year long and strive to advance in that one sport. They hope for the scholarship, or their parents do. Parents hire coaches and send their kids to sports camps.

I could dump a bunch of statistics here that support what I am saying, but let me ask this of you instead. First, think back to playing sports in your own childhood. Now go to a local park and watch kids playing some organized sport. Really look at them. Do they look like they are having fun? Watch what is going on. Watch the action. Would you want to do what they are doing? Is that what sports was like for you? For the most part, I think not. Here is one statistic. Most kids who aren't really good at a sport by age 11 quit because they can't compete. COMPETE, not play – compete. Fun is not the main motivation for kids to play sports anymore, and neither is hanging out with other kids. They play to excel.

Here is an illustration worth thinking about: When I was growing up, my parents would tell me that I had to stay in my room and study instead of playing ball. Today's parents are telling their kids that they can't stay inside on the computer because they have to go to soccer practice. What is wrong with this picture?

5. Minor League Baseball tells us we need more of each other.

Baseball is no longer America's favorite sport, the National Football League now holds that distinction, but in the '50s and '60s baseball was every bit as big as the NFL is today. Baseball built an organization with major – and minor – league conferences that have been unrivaled in attendance ever since. There are more opportunities by far to go to a professional baseball game than any other sport.

But MLB isn't king, the NFL is.

Baseball ruled the '50s with both the major and the minor leagues. The longstanding attendance record for Minor League Baseball was set in 1949 at the height of baseball's reign. That record was broken in 2004, and has continued to be broken every year since.[3] Minor League Baseball is a message to us about the need for Simple Community. Those records are impressive, but made all the more so by the fact there are half as many teams today than there were in the '50s. The fact that there were neither advertising nor marketing campaigns, nor a major national effort to build interest in Minor League Baseball makes it only more impressive. To borrow from the baseball film Field of Dreams, "They didn't build it, we still came." Americans in need of more Simple Community saw the bright lights on summer nights and went to the game. They saw their neighbors there. They didn't need to fight for parking or take out a loan to buy a ticket. It wasn't such an investment that they felt obligated to stay for the whole game. They could come for a while, for as long as it felt good, and then go home. It could be spontaneous. It could be fun with no strings attached.

Perhaps more than any other trend in sports, Americans gathering to cheer for Minor League Baseball teams around the country illustrates that we need more. We want more. We are trying to be part of Simple Community.

Oh, by the way, the end of Field of Dreams is a tearjerker. People come from all over America just to visit a baseball field in a cornfield in Iowa because they long for the dreams of simple pleasure that baseball represents. The producers actually built a field in Iowa for the film, which was made in 1987. People, indeed, did come. They drove to Iowa to see the field. They still come – over 65,000 in 2005[4] – to see an empty field that speaks to the dream of Simple Community. If we build it, they WILL come!

6. Research tells us we need more of each other.

I know of dozens of studies of American perceptions of social needs that have found time with family and friends at the top of the list. I present just two here. Chart 1 is from a study I did in 2005. I asked Americans to choose which category best described their favorite way to spend free time. Their favorite, by far, was spending time with their family and friends. Since I first measured how people prefer to spend their time, starting in the late 1990s, every study has shown that people appreciate time with their family and friends the most.

Favorite Leisure Activities
Percent saying this is their favorite

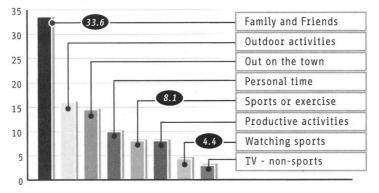

	Family and Friends
	Outdoor activities
	Out on the town
	Personal time
	Sports or exercise
	Productive activities
	Watching sports
	TV - non-sports

CHART 2:

Outdoor Activity is the Biggest Leisure "Desire Gap" in America

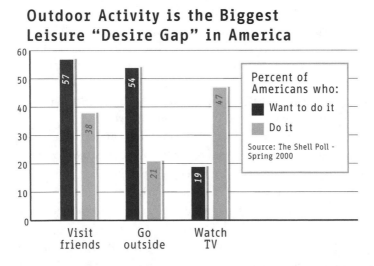

Percent of Americans who:

■ Want to do it

■ Do it

Source: The Shell Poll - Spring 2000

Visit friends   Go outside   Watch TV

Chart 2 is from a survey conducted in 2000 by the Shell Oil Company. First, rather than asking people what they actually do, they asked people what they would do if they had more time. Spending time with family and friends was number one; being outside was second. There were many other ranked options. Only 19 percent said they would watch more TV.

Then the Shell Poll asked respondents what they actually do in their free time. Watching TV came in first. Spending time with family and friends placed second, but there was a "Desire Gap." That is to say, many more people wanted to engage in the activity than were actually doing it. Although 57 percent wanted to spend time with friends, only 38 percent were.

Summary of six things that tell us we need more of each other:

- When weather takes away our technology and we find ourselves unexpectedly face-to-face with our neighbors, we are reminded how much we like it.

- With our homes and downtowns we are inviting others to be more a part of our lives.

- Our past experiences, like picnics, remind us of what we are missing.

- The way today's parents played until the street lights came on reminds us of more engaged neighborhood life.

- The current boom in attendance to minor league sports like baseball – motivated by people's desire, not by marketing campaigns – suggests Americans are already trying to recapture Simple Community.

- Research consistently finds Americans want time with family and friends more than any other free time activity.

It may not seem like we are spending less time enjoying each other's company because we are rarely alone. But if you really think about it, most of that time is spent working on something, not simply enjoying each other. It took me more than a decade of repeatedly seeing the results from my own research before I could understand why Americans are looking to get more out of their friendships and families.

Unfortunately the loss of enjoyable time with others doesn't demand that we stop to fix it. Sometimes I even think we are unconsciously trying to destroy Simple Community because it doesn't produce a tangible good. Has play become a four-letter-word in America? Are we so focused on getting things done that we actually feel guilty about enjoying time with people when there is no to-do list to accomplish? I am afraid that being friendly and living as friends has gone beyond being ignored and is now at the point of unintentionally being considered counter-productive.

I have to confess a seeming contradiction. The solution is simple. How we lost Simple Community is not. There are many different factors that have come together in something of a perfect storm. Some factors, like the change in how most Americans work, took literally hundreds of years to develop. Others, like the economic decline of 2008, took months.

There is no magic to the order in which these factors are presented in the book. At the same time, I have put a lot of thought into how all these dynamics fit together. There are at least half a dozen concepts in Simple Community that will be new to you. I don't present them as truth, just as the best way I know to organize a bunch of complex dynamics to make the case for seeing pleasurable time with others as more important.

Not all of the factors affect everyone the same way. After years of presenting a variety of these dynamics to groups and individuals I have discovered that different dynamics illustrate and prove the need for different people. I present them all with the hope that one or more will apply to you. Hopefully an intentional look at the things that keep us apart will convince us that we need to do something about the loss of Simple Community. The hard part is seeing the problem. Once the problem is clearly seen, it should become easy to start rebuilding.

So what should you expect from reading this book? My greatest hope is that you will find a new desire to do more little things to extend community around you, simple things like sharing the book with a friend or inviting friends or family to do something fun. Maybe you will want to take it a step further. I have included thoughts and stories that I know have motivated audiences when I speak. I hope those sparks can ignite Simple Community through this book as well.

You no doubt noticed the book has two front covers and no back cover. I don't mean this to be a gimmick. There are two fronts because there are two different goals. Living Simple Community was written to help readers appreciate the impact of the loss of time with family and friends on their own lives and to encourage them to make more time for Simple Community. Building Simple Community was written primarily for those who, through their jobs, have the places to gather or resources to make gathering more enjoyable. It is about how you can enhance gathering through your work.

Simple Community
Simply Defined

So far, I have written mostly about a general sense of what is missing. Let me be more specific. Simple Community is not a new concept. In fact, it is so common that it is taken for granted. I define it here so we can consciously consider the ingredients necessary to encourage more. Let me illustrate with a story about friends at a backyard barbeque:

He didn't think about the good he was doing while he flipped burgers for a bunch of neighbors in his backyard. He never meant it as an act of building community. He just felt like being with his friends. He did intend to fix the wobbly leg on the picnic table before anyone got there, but he didn't get around to it.

The gathering was one of those magical moments when everything comes together: great weather, good times, and great conversation. Everyone there knew it was special and worth repeating.

Who would have thought that a leaning neighbor and a bowl of coleslaw would bond a neighborhood together for more than 20 years? They were all talking when the neighbor leaned on the table and the whole thing collapsed, leaving her sitting on the ground covered with coleslaw.

She hosted the neighbors a month later. Three brought big bowls of coleslaw. A tradition was born. Coleslaw continued to be served and its story was revived every time the neighbors gathered – the first Saturday of every summer month – just as it was the first time the picnic table collapsed.

Simple Community is PEOPLE taking TIME to gather together in a PLACE suited to enjoying each other. They bring the RESOURCES needed to have fun. The best times give rise to STORIES that they tell again and again. When they are really lucky, something happens that creates a TRADITION, which begs to be repeated.

These are the six ingredients of Simple Community.

People who have the time to build Simple Community are the ones who kindle the fire. As long as you stick to small gatherings like backyard barbecues, gathering as a group is relatively easy, but the bigger the group or activity becomes, the harder it is to organize. Places and resources are required to build it. Stories are the evidence that Simple Community lives. Traditions are small, silly things often born of completely unintended circumstances, which happen at a time when people are doing things they love. It doesn't get much better than that. And it really is as easy as that.

PART TWO:
How We Lost Simple Community

The decline of Simple Community was the product of a decades-long perfect storm. The four components of the storm were:

- The changing nature of change itself,
- The explosive development and proliferation of personal computing and other new technology,
- The impact of America's transition from an agricultural, to a manufacturing, to a service-based economy, and
- The rise of perhaps the first true generation gap in America in the early 2000s.

Any of these components alone would most likely not have been enough to fracture social life or stunt Simple Community. However, the four together had an overwhelming, unconscious, and unintended result. We don't have an enemy. The closest thing to an enemy would be a lack of awareness of the problem in the first place. We didn't lose meaningful social engagement or community by frontal assault. It was lost as a byproduct of mostly natural and generally positive change.

As if the loss of community over time wasn't enough, in 2008 Americans experienced the worst economic conditions since the Great Depression, nearly eighty years earlier.

What follows is an examination of each of the four components that led to the loss of Simple Community and a discussion of the impact of the economic crisis of 2008. My intent is to spark an awareness of what we lost, how we lost it, and why we need it so much – particularly now – so that we can understand where we are and do something about it.

Change Changed

hange changed. Massive changes like electricity, indoor plumbing, the telephone, and the car came decades apart and took years to become a part of everyday life. Even the fax machine with its explosive adoption rates in the 1980s was slow in coming. It was first developed in 1940.[5] Going to the moon allowed us to realize the scope of our potential and opened doors to technological developments that have yet to be fully realized. The most important aspect of all these advances, though, is that with each innovation, our potential for change increases. That is to say, with each advance, the next one comes even more easily and more quickly. The rate of change is changing, and it is getting extremely fast.

These days, before we have fully come to appreciate the benefits of a major new development, the next change is upon us. We can feel the speed in every part of our lives. It even plays a role in academic thinking at the theory level. My own graduate education is an excellent example.

The graduate program at The University of Michigan that I went through was essentially a dual doctoral program administered by the Department of Communication. In addition to communication, every doctoral student was required to have a second area of mastery. I chose to combine psychology and communication because my interest was the role of media in adolescent social development.

In psychology, although new theories emerge from time to time, they continue to rely on the relative stability of the human condition. Mediated communication theory pretty much has to start from scratch with each new development in communication technology. Around the time that journalism researchers felt they understood print, radio was taking off. Before researchers could form a basis for understanding the impact of radio on propaganda programming, television started to take root. Communication researchers had the decades of the '60s and '70s to consider the role that violence on TV was playing on aggression – devoting only little time to the impact of film – at which point the personal computer and Internet started to become a part of

everyday American reality. I could fill pages with the list of things that have been developed in communication technology since that time. Change is taking place faster than we are able to understand its consequences.

The impact of information overload

I was walking into my favorite breakfast restaurant one morning and encountered the front pages of two local papers. I looked twice.

On the left, the Detroit News declared: "Deficit pinches U-M sports," on the

right, the Ann Arbor News reported: "U-M athletics surplus foreseen." Two reputable papers, both with access to the same information, had arrived at opposite conclusions. I doubt you are shocked by this revelation. Maybe you are thinking something like "Ok. So...?" The issue wasn't the discrepancy, but rather the information overload that it illustrated. We are overwhelmed. Deluged. It is impossible to keep track of all the information being produced. The consequence is that even the ridiculousness of blatantly contradictory headlines passes as one drop in a thunderstorm.

There was a time, not many years ago, when a discrepancy in headlines would have been discussed and dissected for weeks by readers, journalists, academics, maybe even lawyers. Information was far more limited, even scarce, then. In those days, every word of an article was scrutinized and double and triple checked for accuracy. Every fact was verified.

Times have changed. There is just too much information. It is impossible to keep up. We are so overwhelmed that we don't even try. I wanted to get a sense of just how overwhelmed we are, so I committed some time to researching information access and use. I found one particular study that stunned me.[6] It was on the information that people use to make major decisions regarding things like changing careers, choosing a college, or buying a home or a car. The central finding was that for every useful piece of information that a person considered in their decision-making process, there were 17 additional pieces of useful information that they missed. That was not what stunned me. The stunner was that the study was done in 1974. And as near as I can tell, that was the last time such a study was even remotely possible.

As part of my doctoral dissertation, I was expected to do an exhaustive literature review on the role of media in adolescent social development. Being exhaustive demanded that I read everything pertaining to my thesis. The results were reported in the literature review chapter found in every dissertation. I wrote my dissertation in the mid-1980s, which I suspect was near the end of the time the exhaustive requirement was assumed. Exhaustive is still possible today, but only if you choose such a narrow topic that few would choose to study it. There is so much information out there that it has become extremely difficult, if not impossible, to take all the relevant facts into account when making a decision.

Explosive change means WE DON'T HAVE TIME TO THINK before the next new thing is upon us. Currently, our attention is so focused on technological advances, consequent changes, and their affects on our future, that we are not noticing other, more subtle, changes. I hope your reading of Simple Community to this point is refreshing in that regard. I hope this book provides a moment of relief from the rocket speed of change. I hope the refreshment energizes you to start thinking about what might be seeping away from the Simple Community we once had.

Ah, but in the possible event you are not convinced, here are a few more examples of explosive change.

■ Nike products

I was having lunch several years ago with a Nike executive in Nike's cafeteria in Beaverton, Ore. The conversation lagged for a moment. Looking to fill the gap, I asked a simple question: "How many new products will Nike put out in a year?" He asked whether I meant products or variations on the theme. I didn't realize it was a complex question. I kept it simple: Products. So if they put out a new shirt and it comes in several colors that is one product, not several. Ok, he said, that would be about 2,000. TWO THOUSAND?!? I was thinking maybe 10 or 20, even a hundred, but 2,000? I sat there running the math through my head. Two thousand per year over 10 years would be 20,000 products in the store. No way. Next question: How long are new products offered from the time they are first on the shelf until they are no longer offered at retail? About 90 days. Ninety days! Note: Next time you see a Nike product you like, buy two!

■ Sixty thousand new books published annually in the US

This is what I am up against in writing this book. In the United States alone, over 60,000 new books will be published this year.

■ Rollerblades and Razor scooters

Inline roller skates were around in the 1920s but were overtaken in popularity by four-wheel roller skates in the 1950s and '60s. In1983 Rollerblades reintroduced inline skates. It took roughly three years for the craze to mature into a booming market, to take off, then stabilize into the market it is today. About five years later, someone modified the old foot-powered scooter and created the Razor, which retailed for about $50. It took less than a year from the time it was introduced until it was "the" holiday gift at Christmas – along with two or three other competitors.

■ One hundred million websites

You know how most commercial websites work. You go to the home page, and from that page you can click on links that are connected to many more related pages. Toward the end of 2006, the one hundred millionth website was created – website, not web page.

In 2007 there were over 75 million monitored blogs[7] (informal communication sites that cover a specific topic). "Monitored blogs" means they are getting enough hits for their content to be picked up by search engines.

■ *Cell phones and carbon copies*

Have you noticed the technology on your cell phone is obsolete long before your service contract obligation expires? I wonder how many years – probably not many – it will take before someone reading this book asks, "What's a cell phone?" Before you scoff at my exaggeration, consider the following story:

After speaking at a conference about the speed of change, an IBM marketing executive approached me to share his own experience on the subject. He said that his daughter, who was an excellent student, came home from school one day in clear distress. When he asked her what was wrong, she explained that she was going to fail her class and there was nothing she could do about it. Her teacher had given her a paper assignment and said it was to be returned with three carbon copies. The father asked her what the problem was. Her response, "What's a carbon?" For years, he said, IBM's bread-and-butter was the Selectric typewriter, and his own daughter didn't even know what a carbon copy was (For those who don't know, they are paper copies made from typewriter impressions using carbon paper).

I hope that you are now fully aware of how fast things are changing. But, keep in mind that a component of change is subtlety. We don't notice it until it has happened. Although I provided examples in which some aspects of change are obvious, I did not yet address how it is affecting the big-picture or Simple Community. In order to adequately realize those affects, we first need to take a look at a few more aspects of the foundation that we are living on today.

Paying too much attention to technology

When was the last time you were faced with a problem and you asked yourself: "How can I fix this with a car?" Yet today we regularly think of the Internet, personal computing tools and other new technology first when we are looking for an answer. There was a time when we felt the same way about running water, electricity, and the telephone. We over-think innovation during the "attention" phase, the time during which innovations take hold and spread their roots.

My family recently got into a discussion about innovation. We were trying to identify the differences between the impact of automobiles and computers – or technology. Someone suggested that all innovations are technological in nature. If technology is the practical application of science, then to call the current era of innovation the "technology era" would not be very helpful. Instead I will

identify it as the era of personal computing. Certainly, there are applications of technology beyond personal computing. A case could be made for calling this the era of communication technology. Both would be fine for our purpose, but the point is that we are paying too much attention to innovation at the expense of personal interaction.

Personal computing can solve many, but not every problem. And it certainly cannot build Simple Community. The same gut feeling that tells me we need more Simple Community says that we are paying too much attention to technology.

In order to understand how we think about personal computing today and how we can bring balance to the way we think about it in the future, I studied the history of several innovations. By comparing the discovery, development, and adoption of each innovation, I found that, from the time when it is discovered or created until the time when it becomes mainstream, we have three sequential responses to an innovation: anticipation, attention, and acceptance. I will illustrate the responses with the history of the automobile. Not because it is the best support for my findings, to the contrary, it is not a tidy fit. But I think the logic holds and the analogy serves as a reminder that we cannot find a formula for life.

The automobile and our sequential responses to innovation

There are over 600 million cars in the world today – one car for every 10 people. By contrast, in 1900 there were over 175,000 horses in New York City, so many that daily barges were required to bring in food and remove manure. It is tempting to think that automobiles were the cause of the end of the horse-and-buggy era. That would be wrong. Bicycles were the rage for two decades before the car became mainstream. In fact, paved roads came before the car and in response to the needs of bicyclists. So to begin with, the seismic shift caused by transportation and attributed to the car was actually started by the use of bikes, which allowed people to venture farther from home during a day than they had previously realized was possible.

ANTICIPATION:

A culture begins its anticipation response to an innovation only after the change is real and the word is getting out. In the case of the automobile, although the first successful steam car may date back to as early the 1600s in China,

Americans didn't realize that the automobile was a part of their future until more than 200 years later. The first gasoline car, produced by George Seldin in 1877, marks the beginning of the anticipation response to automobiles in America – nearly 30 years before Henry Ford introduced the Model T, which caused the beginning of the "attention" response.

Until an innovation is real, we are dreaming. We are not yet anticipating. Once anticipation begins, though, we are no longer wondering whether it will work; we know it will. It is only a matter of time before we expect it to "Change everything." During anticipation, some people think about the potential applications of the innovation, while for others it is the hot topic at parties. But, everyone who knows about it senses that life will change, and they are eager to learn what that change will entail.

The key aspect of the anticipation phase is that it is the time during which people learn about the innovation. It used to take decades to bring innovations to market. Just think of the effort it took to wire the United States for electricity or to develop indoor water systems. Cable penetration in America is still not 100 percent complete. The key here is that people used to gather information about innovations throughout the anticipation phase, so that, by the time an innovation was actually available, people had a relatively developed concept of what it was they were dealing with. Contrast that with the wildfire penetration of wireless technologies in previously third-world countries or with how quickly high-speed internet spread once fiber-optic cable had been laid across the oceans.

One reason that adoption happens so quickly these days is because each new innovation adds another brick to the foundation for the next change. As we continue to innovate, the amount of additional infrastructure required for individual changes decreases. New innovations pave the way for more and more changes, which are being developed increasingly fast. That certainly wasn't the case with the car. Anticipation of the automobile was fairly long and benign – more than a dream state, but not enough to make any active plans to sell the horse.

ATTENTION:

By 1902 Ransom Eli Olds had a production line and cars were showing up regularly. By then, the odds that you had seen a car were good and your thinking needed to change. Now, rather than just thinking "This will change everything," the more concrete, "Soon, I will have a car," needed to be addressed.

We begin to pay attention when we start coming into direct contact with people

who have the innovation. The attention response has three main components:

■ *When and how will this affect me?*

When the first person on the block got a car, neighbors took turns going for a ride. The car was the center of discussion and social action. People paid attention. They thought about when they might get one, how they would use it, how much it would cost, what it would replace, and how else it would affect their life personally. Trying to figure out when and how the car will be a part of everyday life is one way of paying attention.

■ *How might this hurt me?*

Not all the discussion was favorable. Many people were slow to buy because, at first, Henry Ford's bankers didn't back him, thinking the automobile would be a passing fad. Others were afraid of cars or didn't like them because they scared the horses. They were physically hard to drive, dirty and loud. Not much about owning a car was easy.

While we are fascinated with big new things and pay attention to them, there is still the fear of the unknown. What we don't know can hurt us. Major innovations change lives. It is hard to imagine all the changes being good. So we start asking "What if…" questions. "What if it explodes?" "What if it breaks down miles from home?" "What if I lose control?" We just don't know. So we weigh the pros and cons. The consideration of potential negatives is one way of paying attention.

■ *What else can I do with this?*

Because of cars, we have motels, gas stations, parking lots, traffic signs, outdoor advertising, drive-through services, auto dealers, repair shops, highways, traffic laws, suburbs, weekend getaways, same-day trips to other cities, and more. All these related changes lead to new business opportunities, which allowed entrepreneurially minded people to constantly develop extensions of the automobile. People paid attention to those too. Life continued to change, as Americans continued to respond with intent attention. Considering new possibilities was at the heart of major innovation and a powerful way that entrepreneurs in America paid attention to the growth of the auto industry.

Having a car indeed changed many things. It changed how far people and things could be moved, how fast, and how often. It changed where we stayed when we traveled: motels. It changed where we ate: roadside cafes. It changed the

functional size of the city: the distance from home that could be easily traveled every day of the week.

With all that change, America paid attention to the role of the automobile. When the attention response is that strong, people don't realize that things unrelated to the innovation are still there and are just as important as before. We become like children with new toys, who briefly forget all their other favorites. All things seem possible. Everything seems changed.

During the attention response phase of any innovation, it helps to step back and reflect on life before and after the most recent "big thing" innovation. We are in the heart of the attention phase with new technologies. We often look to computers or communication technology to solve unrelated problems.

How do we feel now about the car? Is it among the first things you think of when a problem arises? Probably not. But I bet the thought "I wonder if I can figure out how to solve this online" is probably right there.

ACCEPTANCE:

Perhaps I can live without a phone. I don't want to because phones are convenient and practical. They are tools, just like my car and running water. I take them all for granted. Perhaps I shouldn't, but none of those things is a defining part of my life or relationships for me, because my response to all those innovations has reached the acceptance phase.

If the innovation was already there when you were born, you will accept it as part of life. If you were born after cars were commonplace, they aren't a big deal. If you were born in 1950, you wondered why adults still thought cars were special. If you have never experienced life without a car, by default, you accept it.

The other way to arrive at acceptance is time; we adjust to innovations gradually. This is an instance of subtle change, so I will illustrate it with an example. Notice that, now, when we talk about cars, it is in terms of developments or policy. We need to control them, make them safer and cheaper, and reduce their environmental footprint. When we stop looking at an innovation for its own sake, but instead focus our efforts on managing it, the attention honeymoon is over. Life goes on. Cars get me from point A to point B. That's it.

■ *Personal computing and the three responses*

The dawn of the anticipation response to personal computing was long

before America went to the moon. The earliest computer-like machines were developed in the 1940s and computer-like capabilities were already being applied to jet propulsion in World War II. However, so much of today's gadgets – from microwave ovens to pocket calculators to the personal computer – were derived from the tools needed to get us to the moon. So I will suggest that anticipation began while Americans were watching that first landing. If going to the moon was possible, anything was possible.

We anticipated the personal impacts for a long time, because of the lag between the invention, first use, and adoption of many innovations first used to get to the moon. We had seen new gadgets on television and we knew they were real, but they weren't available to anyone we knew. Neil Armstrong set foot on the moon in 1969. The personal computer was available in 1970, but was not mass produced for seven more years. The Internet was developed in 1973, but was not in common use for another 20 years. The first cell phone call was also made in 1973, which was 20 years before owning and using one was a realistic expectation for many Americans.

I further suggest that cable TV was the bicycle of the technology boom. Cable came before many high-tech advances and dramatically extended the mass media television culture. It was still television – a one-way delivery system of communication – but it clearly suggested that more could follow soon. America started paying especially close attention to personal computing in 1977 with the introduction of the Tandy TRS-80 and the Apple II computer.

Why? Because the hits just kept on coming. Now, no sooner do we buy a new gadget than another one hits the market. Each innovation is better, stronger, more connected, more functional than the one before. It is impossible to keep up with the developments so, of course, WE PAY ATTENTION!

Unfortunately, as you probably gathered from the previous two chapters, the attention we are paying to personal computing and the expectations we have of it have been distracting us from what really matters in life. Instead of thinking and playing so much with the new gadgets, we need to keep aspects of being human in mind that don't change along with innovation. We still have families and friends, and we interact with each other meaningfully – truly become a part of each other's lives – by spending time and doing things together face to face. We may be able to tell stories through mediated technology, but is that really enough? My best stories are not about me. They are about times I have spent with my family and friends. And although computers allow me to share my stories with

people who I am not in the same room with, there really aren't many compelling stories about times when I used a computer.

Amazing personal computing innovations may never end. However, although the change is subtle, we are most likely entering the acceptance phase with regard to personal computing. Soon, we will no longer be fascinated by each new development. They will be no more or less important than indoor plumbing. And once we are no longer focusing our attention on computing innovations, what will we focus it on? Something we anticipate today will take our attention tomorrow. Personal flight is a good candidate. Whatever the next wonderful thing to come along is, no matter how fascinating it is and how much we want to pay attention, we can't forget those fundamental needs that never change. We need to fight for the time and places to be with each other to assure the stories of enduring life continue.

Working in a
Service Economy

During my years with the ESPN Sports Poll, I explored numerous historical factors that might explain or predict the popularity of sports. In the late 1990s I hit the mother lode; I recognized a new way to look at a historic relationship that didn't just help to understand the popularity of a particular sport, but brought to light a much more critical change in American social fabric. The key factor that ultimately led to the loss of Simple Community in America was not whether the economy was up or down, but was determined by the dominant source of work in America.

In our history, there have been three work economies:

- **The agricultural economy**, which started with our nation's birth and ended sometime around the start of the 20th century,
- **The manufacturing economy**, which followed the agricultural economy, and
- **The service-based economy**, which began sometime in the 1970s.

Most discussions about these three forms of economy have a financial focus. This is a discussion of how the way we make money affects our opportunities to be a community.

■ *The Farming Economy:*

In the 1800s, America was a farm-based economy. More than half of everything we produced was related to farming. In those days, families were bigger for a functional reason: the more kids, the more hands to work the farm. Families were together most hours of the day, most days of the week. They spent most of their time on the farm. There were no cars then; just getting to town was a considerable time commitment. It was a natural, easy extension of work to talk with each other, play, and engage with each other. Generation followed generation. Parents passed the traditions and culture of life on the farm on to their children. Let me bring the community-enabling context of the agricultural

economy to light for you. The three most popular sports during that time were barn wrestling, boxing and horse racing.[8] Sports interests emerged naturally as part of the work experience. Can't you just see it?

Brothers Bob and Bill are at the end of a long day on the farm. Toward the end of feeding the horses with hay from the loft, Bob jumps on Bill – all in fun, of course – and a wrestling match is on. Bob always wins. Farm families routinely go to town on Saturdays to get supplies and socialize with their neighbors. Bob's family talks with the family from the other side of the county. Their son John always wins the wrestling matches on their farm. "Yeah? I bet my Bob can beat your John." "You're on." The community gathers and the match is on. A sport is born. "My horse is faster than yours," leads to horse racing. Boxing arises for similar reasons. The context of farm life was integral to the birth, life, and popularity of each sport.

Farming was not just work, not merely a job, but a way of life. For farm families, community activities were naturally attached to the things they had to do to make a living. Most farms were multi-generational – grandparents, parents and kids working together. The farm stayed in the family and was passed down from one generation to the next. In the late 1800s, farming was the only way of life that most people knew. Honored traditions had been developed over generations of consistency, of which Simple Community was a byproduct. It was a whole-life experience – centered on family – built on how people made a living.

A side thought here. I wonder how much of the divorce we see in American culture today is related to the fact families no longer need to work together to make ends meet. I wonder if during the farming era we thought of family being at the heart of our cultural roots because the first generations of America had to work together as families to survive. I wonder how much of the family bond was unconsciously economic as opposed to a consciously adopted value system. I suspect we don't notice the loss of Simple Community today so much because, when we did have it, it was taken for granted and was more a byproduct of paying the bills. Even though it was probably an unconscious benefit back then, we had Simple Community. We sense a loss of something today, but maybe we can't articulate it as Simple Community because, until now, we didn't need to consciously work to have time together. Just a thought.

■ The Manufacturing Economy:

Manufacturing dominated the 1900s. Work was away from home. Cars made it possible for Americans to work farther away. Families and neighbors came

together to work the line. Factory work was restricted to a remote work place, not so much a way of life. But the factory became the heart of what sustained the town. People's town pride and sense of connection came from their link to the factory. Working together still sustained friendships and afforded time for talk and social gathering during breaks and after work. Office work in the 1900s was similar to manufacturing work. People commonly kept a job at one company for an entire career, forming life-long relationships with co-workers that were refreshed by talk around the water cooler – a concept mostly lost on those born since 1980. Children commonly went to work at the same companies as their parents. In as much as that continued from generation to generation, manufacturing work was a way of life too.

In the farming era, community was built around family. When manufacturing dominated the economy, community was built around factories, towns and the neighbors who worked together. Sports continued to be defined by the economy. In the heart of the manufacturing era, baseball was by far the most popular sport. Factories – and by extension the community – took the place of individual families. It was no longer boxing or wrestling that pitted one family's best against another's. Instead, community members rooted for their town. "My Bob can beat your John," became, "Our town's team can beat your town's." The type of economy changed, but it enabled Simple Community nonetheless, by continuing to give rise to activities that naturally brought people together.

■ *The Service Economy:*

By 2000, America was a service-based economy. Service workers provide information, advice, and a variety of other intangible commodities. They do not grow or make things. Most jobs allow people to work alone. People readily change from one job to another and from one company to the next. Technology allows people to work remotely. Writing this book is service work. I can write in my office or at the beach. Service work does not create a real sense of place. Often there is little or no connection with others who do the same job. Few service workers will work for only one company throughout their career. Many not only will change companies, but also will change careers within the service industry. Service work is much more often a job and less often a way of life. Because people don't work in the same place together for a sustained period of time, no consistent social culture is created. Consequently, the contexts that give rise to Simple Community are also diminished.

Farms kept families together in the same way that factories kept neighbors together; they needed to work together to survive. Although work brought people together out of necessity, it also created a natural context in which Simple Community thrived. People didn't have to go out of their way to pay money or set aside time to be together, it was a natural byproduct of their work. They could easily piggyback Simple Community on their time spent working together.

Now that workers are constantly changing tasks, jobs, companies and careers, there are fewer predictable, sustainable times when workers can add Simple Community to the workday. Our service economy does not naturally give rise to the same social benefits that farmers and manufacturers enjoyed.

Being socially connected through work was a cornerstone of American culture for the first 200 years of our history. Simple Community was assumed. To be connected with family and friends required no more than going to work. That assumption is no longer true. That said, Americans still want to be connected. They want Simple Community. It is a top priority – THE top priority. The evidence is in the research and – more importantly – in the realization of people who are grasping at a need for Simple Community that is not being fulfilled.

Sports and the three economies

Sports are neither the biggest nor anywhere near the most important component of life. But there are very few other things that are enjoyed in so many ways by so many Americans of all ages. We only watch TV. We only participate in hobbies. We watch AND participate in sports; we even follow the play of others. Some other aspects of life – like political or religious interests – may have deep involvement, but they tend either to be specific to a time of year or the focus of smaller groups. There is a major sport active in America nearly every day of the year. The most watched television program each year is the Super Bowl. Sports provide literally countless opportunities for families, friends and neighbors to be together. They support decades-long traditions. Because of their reach and depth, sports are telling.

If farming produced farm-based sports and manufacturing produced the popularity of team or geographically based sports (starting with baseball and shifting to football), what should we expect from the service-based economy? The answer is individual sports. Sometime around 2000, I started saying that the NFL wouldn't remain atop the sports world. It will take decades for the change to fully play out, but our service-based economy does not naturally support

professional team sports.

If football falters, what will replace it? Starting in 2001, I suggested poker as a prototype for the future. Of course, at the time, most people thought I was insane: "Poker bigger than the NFL???" No. It will never be as big as the NFL, but it is the type of competition that will rise, shine for a while, and give way to the next. My point was that poker is an individual game, played socially, with a strong Internet element; it is the type of "sport" that is naturally supported by a service-based economy.

Before sports loving readers get depressed, let me modify the analysis slightly. Sports are not the first enterprise to be affected in this way. Television went through a similar transition with the dawn of cable. Before cable, there were three major networks. Cable gave rise to the potential for hundreds of channels. In the 1980s, there were dire predictions that the networks would die. The networks have not died, but they have given up large shares of audience to cable and other television viewing options. In most cases, the networks still draw significantly larger audiences. But while "I Love Lucy" had more than half of the population tuned in as she led all shows back in the '50s, the top network shows today do well to have 20 percent of America watching.

That's likely to be the case in sports as well. The NFL may reign for decades, but in future years their numbers will decline. Members of the sports industry should already be deeply concerned. Since the start of the ESPN Sports Poll in 1994, the 12-17 year-old male has always been the biggest fan. Since 2003, 18-24 year-old fans have had greater high level interest in sports than the 12-17 year olds. This probably signals the start of the decreased priority of team-based sports as entertainment in America. This transition may also provide a clearer indication of the impact of being a service-based individualized economy. The temptation in the sports industry may be to shore up interest among youth. I suspect that would be addressing a symptom, not the underlying issue. The issue is that the service-based economy no longer supports Simple Community. We need to shore up Simple Community. Then we can see where sports fit into the mix.

The First Real Generation Gap

A s if the speed of change, the explosion of innovation, the advent of the service-based economy, and our attention to new media technology were not enough to take our focus off Simple Community, there is one more human element – different from all the rest – that must be mentioned. This last point of consideration is the introduction of, perhaps, the first real generation gap in American history. Unlike the others, this generation gap is real because it is built on the differences in tool capabilities between the two generations, not social values – the generational issue during the Vietnam War. I want to introduce yet another new way of looking at things. I call it generational DNA.

Two major types of change can affect our life. There are historical changes (9/11, Katrina, war, economic depressions, etc.) and innovative changes (electricity, cars, etc.). Both kinds of changes add generational DNA markers to everyone relative to when they were born. Historical changes impact how we think and feel; Innovative changes impact what we do and how we do things.

First, let's examine historical changes. History has a mind of its own. History happens. Though some may try, it is hard, if not impossible, to cause an intended historical outcome. We can't predict how people and events will respond. Most things that turn out to be historically significant were not designed specifically to alter our day-to-day lives.

Nevertheless, historical changes usually alter our thinking and feeling. Positive changes tend to be rarer and more gradual. Over time, we may experience an improving economy, declining crime statistics, and growing consumer confidence. The thoughts and feelings that accompany good times are ones of greater security and the simple desire to come out of our shells – or bomb shelters – and re-engage in the open. The impact of negative historical change is the opposite. We become more fearful, sheltered, and retreat into our shells.

As for innovative changes, they are mostly tool innovations or changes that dramatically improve what we do or how we do it. Nearly always these changes are seen as positive and welcomed. Examples include the obvious: indoor plumbing, electricity, the automobile and the Internet.

Generational DNA markers

Historical or innovative changes that took place before a person was born are considered part of their generational DNA. They are part of what defines the person, whether they think about them or not. I was born with the automobile in my generational DNA, so I didn't walk outside today looking to saddle the horse. Americans living today would never think to light the kerosene lamp in a house. Cars and electricity are part of our DNA. They are part of life – assumed, not thought about or optional.

When an historical or innovative change occurs during one's lifetime, it results in options. Multi-tasking and the Internet were around in my mother's later years, but neither really touched her. Both affected her interactions with others, but only to a limited extent. The world changed around her, but she didn't change with it. There is a massive difference between being born into a changed world and having the world change while you are living. Americans born in 1970 cannot live without a phone – but they can take or leave the Internet. Someone born in 1990 can live without a landline – but not without a cell phone or the Internet.

Sometime in the early 2000s the baby boomer generation gap ended. Sadly, the end came mostly because the boomer's parents were dying. As I mentioned earlier, that generation gap was more imagined than real. If you asked kids in the '60s if they or their parents knew more about life, the kids would say they did. Ask the parents and they would say that they did. Being a child of the '60s, I now admit the parents knew more. Today a much more powerful generation gap has emerged which is neither emotional nor value laden. Both generations are largely unaware it even exists. The gap is not based on historical changes but on innovative changes. It is a real gap. And it is a real problem.

Something as simple as a power outage in a thunderstorm in 1984 could have signaled the birth of the new generation gap. The crisis centered on a video cassette recorder. The clock on the VCR was flashing 12:00 and the parents in the house didn't have a clue what to do. Any self-respecting parent just found the nearest eight-year old to set the clock. Perhaps you chuckled. I hope so. But there is a bigger issue underneath this story that has much broader implications. Those born since 1984 have the Internet and many other new media technologies as part of their generational DNA. Their parents do not. The parents can take it or leave it. For the most part, they leave it to their kids. These new innovations, contrary to the beliefs of many parents, are of course not merely toys. They are

the tools of the future.

I would wager a healthy sum that the following is true: Most high school students take classes that require learning some aspect of technology. If you tested the students' and the teacher's knowledge of the uses of the technology before the semester began, many, if not most, of the students would already know more than the teacher. The point is, today kids think they know more about the tools of the future and they are probably right.

The book, *The Dumbest Generation*,[9] published in 2008 suggests that high school students and graduates from the 2000s are the least educated ever. The author, Mark Bauerlein, bases his conclusion on their inability to answer simple questions about current events, history or geography. His assumption is that knowledge and education are measured by what we carry around in our heads. It is a faulty assumption and at the heart of the current generation gap. His generation did not have today's information technology, so people had to learn and retain knowledge. Smart people were defined by what they remembered. In those days, people were an inch wide and a mile deep in knowledge. Bauerlein might think that today's kids are a mile wide and an inch deep. He would have to conclude that the "lack of depth" – the absence of memorized facts – equals being dumb. However, today's kids are a world wide and an inch deep. But they have the information tools needed to go to the core of the Earth on any issue. Why remember something when, in less than 30 seconds, you can find it with authority?

In past generations, the adult taught the child how to prepare for the future and use the tools required for basic survival and success. Now, for the first time, the kids are setting the clocks. The sobering reality is that we have an entire generation that is essentially without mentors. The implications are obvious. Of course kids have reservations about asking their parents or teachers about advice on careers, school, marriage, religion, and politics. Look at it from their perspective, "You can't even set a clock. How could you possibly help me to prepare for the future?"

Another major difference between kids and adults today is their perspective on resources and need. My mother-in-law lived through the depression. In the 1970s I saw her take a bite out of a cookie and put the rest of it on a shelf in the cupboard. I looked at her quizzically and she said "Oh Richie, you never know..." She conserved everything because she had lived through times when a whole cookie was a luxury. Those times had been over for decades, but they remained

in her generational DNA. In 2008, the youngest generation has no concept of real need. They can seemingly get anything and everything at any time they want it. While the oldest generation thinks in terms of "I had better have a good reason for buying it," the youngest thinks in terms of "I want it "or "I don't."

This generation gap, built on real tool differences and considerably different decision-making thought frames, is very real. Like our diminishing ability to be involved in Simple Community, it is not a result of a single cause. Rather, it is the net result of many major historical and innovative changes happening quickly and at the same time. Until about 1960, essential changes affecting generational DNA happened infrequently enough that they never caused a gap. Americans were not adjusting to automobiles while getting used to computers. So when it came to relationships and understanding each other, there wasn't a pressing need to consider the discrepancy in generational DNA. Now, most kids are correct in assuming that their parents are unable to offer advice about the tools they will need for the future. Their extended assumption that parents are unqualified to give them guidance about other parts of life is understandable – generally wrong – and tragic.

Earlier, I mentioned that my dissertation was about the role of media in adolescent social development. When I did the research in the '80s, the media were mostly television, film and music. At the time of the research there were no psychological theories of development that took media impact into account, so I had to create a new model. I relied heavily on the best existing theories and research of the time from both psychology and communication to arrive at, and successfully test, the following theory.[10]

Adolescents who have a good relationship with one or both of their parents are more confident and have a better ability to form friendships. Adolescents who have at least one good friend are more likely to form a group of friends. When a kid has all three – a good relationship with a parent, a friend, and a group of friends – he or she is able to try out a very broad range of adult-like activities to see how it goes. The people in his or her life provide real feedback – usually without hurt feelings being involved – that helps the kid to move closer to the courage, hopefully mixed with excitement, to take on adult life. These well-adjusted kids watch TV as entertainment, knowing that what they are watching doesn't match the reality of what they are living. For well adolescents, reality always beats media. At most, media enhances their view of reality, it rarely, if ever, forms its basis.

On the other hand, if a kid does not have a strong relationship with a parent, that kid will be less likely to have the courage and ability to form a strong friendship. The absence of that friendship nearly always means that the kid will not become part of a group of friends. These kids end up being socially isolated. They don't have contexts for trying adult behavior. They don't have a blueprint for what to expect or how others will react to them. For socially isolated kids, the media often function as that blueprint. They see how adults act on TV and assume that those actions resemble reality. When the media perspective is realistic, it serves as a good model. When it isn't, and it often isn't, reality jars the adolescents who try to copy the blueprint it provides.

Let me give one illustration: sexual behavior. Ideally, reality would suggest sex has warm personal connection and relationship as an integral part of it. Clearly, sex also produces children. In reality, without care, sex can produce disease. The dominant blueprint in the media is that sex is about elation and is for immediate personal pleasure without consequence. If an isolated adolescent has that frame, they are in for a rude awakening, an awakening with the potential to affect their long-term development.

The good news from my research is that more than 85 percent of the kids I studied had sufficiently adjusted lives and relationships to base their perception of the world on reality. That having been said, the remaining kids who have deficient experiences or are isolated are still too many.

The point is this. My dissertation was before the Internet and so-called social networking. The ability to be more disconnected or remote in adult experimentation may make it easier for kids today to avoid relationships with adults. I see studies and hear from those born before 1980 that they are communicating more with their parents now than kids did twenty years ago. Adolescents love their parents and stay in touch. That is great. However, we cannot ignore the diminished capacity for adults to prepare their children for the future. The kids have the tools that they need for work, but there is so much more to life that they don't have. Unless both the adults and the kids come to an awareness and appreciation of their need for each other, this could be one painfully long generation gap that is silent on the most important issues.

Kids have the tools for the future. They need the love! They aren't aware of what they are missing. The more adults do to enable Simple Community, the more and richer experience they will be providing for kids to prepare them for adulthood.

Do something about it. Simple Community begins at home and in your

neighborhood. It begins simply.

Would you be interested in giving your son our daughter a memory that will last a lifetime? Ask them to go for a walk with you. Invite time with no agenda, no plan, and when it is just the two of you. Don't schedule it. Don't make it a long ordeal – no 10-mile hikes. Don't lead a discussion. A walk around one block with no words said may be the best relational gift you give. By resisting the temptation to turn this into an agenda you send the message: "I want to spend time with you." As a bonus, if you don't start the discussion, your child might start it instead. Wouldn't that be wonderful?

If you want to do something meaningful for other kids in your neighborhood, reach out, start a conversation. Ask how they are enjoying high school or what their interests are. Speak to them as one adult to another. Provide them with an opportunity to try on the grown-up shoes that came to you more naturally through Simple Community.

Additionally – but never as good as being with them – we can relate better to the younger generation by learning how to use a computer. They will certainly communicate more with us if we know how to text message or instant message on computers. Whenever I teach undergraduate classes, I randomly stop the class sometime during the semester and ask how many students have communicated with a parent during that class period. I started doing that in 1999. There has always been at least one, which is wonderful.

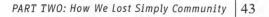

The Economy

I wrote the first draft of this section in the spring of 2008 before the bottom fell out of the economy. We should have seen this coming. It shouldn't have surprised us. The greatest economic pressure at that time was the impact that gasoline prices were having on disposable income. The first of the banks caught up in the mortgage crisis had yet to come to light.

+++ Spring, 2008

I believe America is headed into the most difficult economic time of at least the past 50 years. There is no way to know how bad it will get. For the first time in years, Americans are actually driving less in spite of there being millions more drivers. Unlike the recession blips of years past, this one is cutting to the bone. I mention it here because economic difficulty magnifies the need for Simple Community. You may be reading this book long after I wrote it. Hopefully this time has passed without tremendous pain. Somehow I doubt that will be the case. Of this much I am sure: More Americans are feeling the pain today than are not. There are two different problems.

■ *PROBLEM ONE:*

Every day the newspaper adds to the economic gloom.[11] There was a mortgage crisis at the end of 2007 that led to 53 percent more home foreclosures compared to the previous year – which was also a bad year. Gasoline was over $4 per gallon. Home energy prices had risen by twenty or more percent. The increased fuel prices caused all modes of transportation to dramatically increase charges. Delivery of goods was becoming far more costly and those costs were driving up costs of goods and bringing inflation – wholesale prices were up over nine percent since June 2007. The dollar was extremely weak– down 13.2 percent against the Euro over the course of the previous year. Blue-chip stocks had declined over 21 percent, signaling a bear market. America was spending billions on the Iraq war.

What does information like this mean to the average American?[12] A little over half of American households made less than $50,000 per year in 2008. Those households averaged less than $3,000 per year in discretionary income – money

they could spend after all their bills were paid. Simply put, the increase of the cost of gasoline all but wiped out money for non-essentials. If gas didn't do it, other increases did.

That means that most Americans have been left with three choices for what they do in their free time: spend no money on it, borrow money (credit card debt) to cover it, or hold off needed expenses such as clothing or repairs to cover the cost of desired products or experiences like vacations.

Thinking of building Simple Community, here is a natural fit: People have to eat, people go to parks. It costs little or no additional money to pack your meal up and eat in a park – it's called a picnic. Take it a step further. Start playing bocce ball and make your picnic a tradition. Rekindle the simpler, less expensive time with loved ones that worked just fine before we got stuck in the attention phase of personal computing.

■ **PROBLEM TWO:**

More than half of America is suffering from the worsening economic conditions, but few of those who control resources that could be used toward relief are responding.

The problem is that most programs that could help must be launched by the people who control the $300 billion dollars spent on advertising, sales and marketing each year in America. Unfortunately, these decision makers make more than $150,000 a year, which means that, on average, their households have more than $20,000 a year available for discretionary spending. Tough as these times are economically, if you are making that much or more, the rough economy has most likely had little or no direct impact on your day-to-day life.

Many American families know how they would like to spend their time, but they don't have the resources. The people with the power and money to make a difference often don't feel the need, and of those that do, many have no idea how hard it is to live with less disposable income than they are used to and therefore aren't taking steps to create meaningful opportunities for others.

———————————————

I added the following section in light of the dramatic changes that occurred in just a few short months.

+++ December 2008

I spent time reading about the Great Depression and looked again at government economic statistics to compare that period with 2008.

The key years of the depression were 1929-1933. In two of those years, 1932 and 1933, the average American spent more money than he made. Those were the only two years since 1929 that was true.

At the same time, the average American family continued to spend between two and three percent of their income on recreation. In 1932-33, even though they couldn't pay all their bills, families continued to spend on fun, on Simple Community. That says to me that Simple Community is a need, not a want. Recreation refuels life to face the hard times ahead. The word recreation itself implies that it is a need. Every time we engage in Simple Community we are "re-creating" our lives. So keep in mind that every dollar spent on Simple Community is recreation spending; it is an investment in a need, not a want.

Few Americans alive today have faced the severity of an economic situation equivalent to the current one. Many of the declines in market and housing values rival the losses of the Great Depression. And as I write, there is no good reason to believe these times will soon end. Therefore, a second great need for Simple Community has been added. Not only do we need it because our work context provides much less of the place, time and resources to gather together. We need relief from what are the most trying economic times Americans have felt in more than fifty years.

PART THREE:
The Solution

Here's what we can do.

No matter who you are, how busy you are, what your talents are, or who you know, there is something you can do to build Simple Community.

Just go out and play! There is no master plan with specific outcomes. If we created complex goals, it wouldn't be simple. In all my years of community building, my greatest enjoyment has come from seeing the results. Stories and traditions will do more to tell you what to build than any planning session could. Ideally, the process begins with someone who has something fun to do and a passion to share it with others.

While not master-planned or complex, there is a little picture and a big picture view of building Simple Community. The little picture is more important than the big-picture. It is anything people do when they get together – like a backyard barbecue. A few people, using readily available resources to have a good time, and enjoying each other's company is the little-picture.

The big-picture is important too. Imagine hundreds of places just waiting for you to come have fun. I had an office in Chicago that overlooked the river near Lake Michigan. At any moment in the summertime, I could look out my window and see literally hundreds of people having a great time for free, because of what the city has done to make places and resources available. There are parks and trees throughout the downtown area and walkways for miles along the lakeshore.

Free concerts are held twice a week in the park. That free concert series is the longest standing series in the country – and it was started during the Great Depression to provide a source of relief!

There are great fireworks every Wednesday and Saturday night. Downtown Chicago looks like a Norman Rockwell painting, because the city invested in the

big-picture – a great place and the resources to make it special.

Imagine what would happen if $30 billion a year were invested in providing places and resources to build the big-picture all over America.

Here is another example of cultivating the big-picture. Nearly every high school in America celebrates homecoming. Decades ago, most homecoming weekends had a parade. On Friday night, the community would attend the homecoming football game, where the focus was on high school, the game, and the football team. On Saturday, the parade provided a different context in which the high school students and the community were closely engaged with each other; the focus was on celebration and on each person being part of the bigger community.

One way to cultivate the big-picture of Simple Community at the high school level would be to reintroduce the homecoming parade. Not every high school would participate, but they could if they wanted to. Every high school and community could take a different approach and have a unique identity. What if we could make resources available to do a parade in every high school in America? That is a big-picture idea that could spark hundreds or thousands of little-picture stories in towns all over America.

To borrow from John Lennon, "You may say I am a dreamer, but I am not the only one." You are still reading. This is not an impossible dream.

Nearly all Americans have to work to pay the bills. To do that, we have a job where we earn money. We are all dependent on others needing the products and services of the companies and organizations that pay us. The United States population has gotten so large and so service-work centered that "work" has become far less personal.

In the farming and manufacturing eras, we were happy to support our friends who ran the stores we bought from. For the most part we didn't question their motives for wanting to sell us things. At some level, it is possible for companies to return to a neighbor mentality in how they do business and provide real good for the people who buy their products and services. Many products and services – such as food, beverages and recreational products, naturally provide the resources welcomed for the purpose of making simple gathering more enjoyable.

We can match the desire of people to be together with the places they can gather and the resources that would make it more enjoyable without exploiting the situation. It starts with people who want to build Simple Community.

Think back to the story of the backyard barbeque that started a tradition

of monthly gathering, and how it illustrated the six ingredients of Simple Community. Now it is time to take a look at those in more detail.

The first two ingredients, People and Time, are the most accessible ingredients. Now that you have realized the need for Simple Community, you will most likely find others with that same need. Setting aside time to be together should come naturally.

The most challenging ingredients to find are Places and Resources. They are available to everyone on the small scale necessary to build the little-picture; however, most people are not in a position to provide these ingredients to an extent that could facilitate building the big-picture. Nonetheless, I will touch on them here.

If you want to build Simple Community and you don't have the places or the resources to host the village, that's still great. Simple Community exists on many levels and it has to start somewhere. As we discussed, a place can be your back yard and a resource can be your grill, so everyone has the ability to begin building Simple Community.

If you are one of the few, or if you know someone, who can provide places or resources to affect change on a larger scale, this chapter will teach you the basics of how to cultivate them to build the big-picture. Flip the book over and read Building Simple Community to learn how.

Finally, there are Stories and Traditions. These cannot be organized, found, or created. They are what tell you that Simple Community is alive and well. Your role, with regard to these two ingredients, is to wait patiently until they evolve naturally and to celebrate and nurture them once they are realized.

People and Time

Two ingredients of Simple Community are available to everyone and have no direct associated cost: people and time.

People:

People are the one relative constant in our world of high-speed change. And in the midst of people are "people-people." They bring us together. They do it without asking, because they want to. They don't do it on assignment. They don't do it as a program. They do it because something inside them says that they want to be with family and friends. They make it happen.

Building Simple Community doesn't start with recruited volunteers. It starts and lives through the passion of determined people. That you have read this far suggests that you are probably one of those people. People are naturally drawn to Simple Community once they come into contact with it, in the same way that people continue to eat ice cream after experiencing it for the first time. The real message of the movie Field of Dreams applies here: "If you build it, they will come." So far, every time I have worked with a group on developing community, someone has stepped up and started building Simple Community activities before we were even finished planning. The right people come out of nowhere. This book is my strategy for finding them.

Inertia: Things in motion tend to stay in motion; things at rest tend to stay at rest. If any part of what you have read thus far has motivated you to move, please move. If you haven't been in motion, take one step. Go for that walk with someone. If you are already in motion – if you have been a people-person for some time – consider the next step. What is one more thing you can do to support Simple Community?

Here are two options for the next step. For some, just the thought of taking another step is overwhelming. Go no further. Do no more. I ask only this of you: keep your eyes open. Listen to the stories that others tell. Be a more conscious observer of life around you. What you are listening for is the sound of another people-person. When you find one, ask yourself if that person is sparking Simple Community. If they don't realize the need and their opportunity, have a conversation with them. This might be the person you

should give this book to when you finish reading it. If it is clear that they are bringing people together for a purpose, think of what would happen if they had more places or resources to work with.

Finally, without starting a movement, if you already know someone who has access to the places or resources to build the big-picture, please keep that person in mind as you read the rest of the book. You may not have the time, energy, or resources to build more Simple Community, but if you know someone who does, then that person is the target for your book giveaway. Overwhelmed or tired as you are, you are investing time to read this book. Thank you. Take one more step and pass it to the next person who can contribute to Simple Community. Then take a nap!

On the other hand, if you are a people-person and have the time and energy to really go after this, pay particular attention to the sections on places and resources. Whether it is you or someone else in your town who controls one or both of those ingredients, keep your eyes open for ways to add to Simple Community. That is a starting point. If you have access to the places and the resources, you can become an ambassador for Simple Community.

What would you start, if you had a great idea about how to build Simple Community and you had access to the places and resources? What would you do at parks or high schools? What fun activity would you facilitate, if all 160 minor-league baseball stadiums were available during a game each summer? Obviously, I am thinking of the extremely big-picture. I doubt you have access to all the minor-league baseball stadiums in the country, but if you did, just think of all the opportunities!

That being said, let's go back to the little picture. Here's an example of building Simple Community if you have a place and the resources:

I was strategizing with a large corporation about what to do with sports events. It was August and it was hot outside. We had been working for three days. Picture us in business attire in a conference room. We hit a lull. I gave them two choices. Either I give them a presentation on the value of Simple Community, or we go outside and have a water balloon fight. Admit it. Just hearing that put a smile on your face. They called my bluff and went for the balloon fight. I HAD THE BALLOONS! I have no idea how many people – a lot – were at their office windows looking outside at a dozen business people getting drenched and laughing in the parking lot!

Simple Community can be that simple. What we are talking about here can

happen anywhere and everywhere. There don't have to be limits. The places and resources exist. Most of us want to get wet! All it takes is for YOU to come up with a fun idea and provide it. Start with the little-picture, all it took for the water balloon fight was the idea, a bag of balloons, and a parking lot. If something stirs you to think about the big-picture after that, then take the initiative to provide or to get access to places and resources on a larger scale.

Time:

"I don't have time." You probably do. We usually think we don't because we are distracted. We are being begged by billions of dollars to buy things. We are trying to filter through phone messages, emails and junk mail. We try to keep one eye open to the daily news. When asked directly, most Americans say that they have two or three hours per day that are not committed to something specifically. Almost 15 percent say that they have no time. However, when measured directly, it turns out Americans have approximately seven to nine hours of free time per day on average. If you account for work (getting ready, commuting each way, and work you do away from work to support work); school (time at school, homework, and commuting); sleep; and chores (the things you do to sustain life like: shopping, cooking, eating, cleaning, paying bills, etc.), you still have a lot of time left over to do the things you want to do.

How can that be? Those must be all the people who aren't working or who are in school – like retired people. Nope. They are included in the self-estimates average, too, and they correctly guess that they have much more time.

Here is what a full-time worker who is "free-time poor" might look like. There are 168 hours in a week.

If a person sleeps eight hours per day:
56 hours per week.

Forty hours per week working and 10 commuting:
50 hours per week.

Three hours per day in chores:
21 hours per week

That leaves just under six hours free time per day:
41 hours per week

Using that same model, if you work ten hours a week more you still have four

free hours a day.

Weekends make a difference. For most Americans, the majority of their free time is on Saturday and Sunday. Five days of the week feel jammed. We push chores to the weekend. We want to relax. The time just slips away. It slips away, but it is there. If you watch all of primetime TV every night during the week, there go 21 hours.

You may be asking yourself whether you are wasting a lot of time. Philosophically – and probably functionally – no, you are not; we decide how we will use every second. We strictly or loosely commit 120-plus hours per week toward activities – or sleep – that will keep us alive. We choose how to spend the rest of those hours. Every time we choose what to do, it was our best choice at that moment. It had to be. That was what we decided to do. We could have done something else, but we didn't.

I encourage you to become more conscious of what you do with your time. Here is a little mechanism to help. I am going to have the audacity to tell you what you treasure more than anything else in life. If you think it is your money, or family, or something else, after this exercise you will know for sure.

I am more beautiful than Marilyn Monroe, more intelligent than Einstein, stronger than Hercules, wiser than Solomon, richer than Howard Hughes. By any other measure of treasure, I defeat them all for one reason. I am alive and they are not. I have time. They don't.

I don't care what you say you treasure most. It doesn't matter where you say your heart is. Show me how you spend your time and I will show you your treasure. If you are floundering in your life and want to assess your priorities, keep a diary of your time in 15-minute increments. Do it for two weeks. Then sort the time into buckets of what you were doing. Add up the total hours for each bucket and put them on a list in order from most to fewest hours. You are now looking at the treasures of your life.

I have to confess to a real irony here. This book has been building in my mind for 10 years. Only recently have I more or less stopped everything to write it. Right now, THIS BOOK is my only treasure. I am in no way practicing what I preach these weeks as I maintain my focus on these thoughts – to my wife Vicki's loss (I think...). Even in 20-hour days writing, I have stopped to watch a movie in the park, walk with my brother, have breakfast with a friend, have drinks with the neighbor, play softball with my co-workers, AND take several

walks by myself in Grant Park or by the Chicago River while I ate a sandwich. It is possible – even in the most intense of schedules – to find time for Simple Community and yourself.

I have more good news for you. You get the same 24 hours every day as everyone else. We all are equal when it comes to the most important treasure on Earth.

Places and Resources

The other side of the book, Building Simple Community, focuses on encouraging the people with the places and resources for building the big picture to make the most of them. For that reason, I address those ingredients on this side of the book only briefly. The aspects of places and resources that are important for anyone who wants to encourage community are included here. For the operational approach and strategies to do more on a big scale, flip the book.

Places:

Because Places are such an important ingredient of Simple Community, I need to explain them in more detail. In their most basic form, they are where people gather. We can build Simple Community one place and one activity at a time. As I mentioned earlier, a backyard can be a place to build Simple Community at the little-picture level: Have a barbecue.

But imagine what would happen if there were thousands of places across America, not just available for Simple Community, but intentionally prepared for and welcoming it.

Some people might want to start building a network of places like that from scratch. The wonderful news is that those places already exist. For example, there are already over 500,000 managed parks in America. We can start by working with the parks people. Parks are a great place to build Simple Community.

What if you want to do more? What if you want to take a little step towards building the big-picture? Imagine you want to start a softball league. People do it all the time. If there are 10 teams with 15 people per team, the league will provide a lot of fun for 150 people. That's great. Let's look at the role of place in making a softball league a reality.

One or two people can easily start a softball league as long as they can rely on two things. First, they need softball fields. No fields, no leagues. We take American parks for granted – kind of like breathing. Parks are everywhere, like sidewalks, which we also take for granted until we hit a part of town where there are none. I digress.

The local parks and recreation department is there specifically to enable Simple

Community. If you are forming a league, just pick up a phone to organize timing, parks, schedules and the rest. The second thing needed to start a league is a group of 150 people. Sometimes the parks and recreation department announces a league and a person only needs to field a team of 15 or be one person joining an existing team. But there are work leagues, neighborhood leagues, church leagues – all formed by one person who knew and had access to an organization of people who would likely play.

In general, 149 of 150 people playing in a softball league can, and do, take for granted that they can play in a softball league if they want to. They assume that somebody will organize it, that there are parks to play on, and that there will be other people.

We can't take places for granted. We also can't always expect those who have the fields to provide the resources to make our softball leagues happen. In December 2008, a common news story covered city services that are drastically cutting back or being eliminated altogether. The true impact of these cuts will not be felt until after Simple Community has been published. Until the economy improves, I suspect in many cases parks and ball fields will still be available but we will be on our own to organize play. I further believe these cuts, while painful in the short term, may be very helpful in the longer term. Hopefully we will not take the places and resources for granted after suffering a significant amount of time without them.

The type of place at which people gather varies. Some are casual, like a porch or backyard; others are very organized, like The Ann Arbor Street Art Fair, which draws 500,000 people every July. Most places are attached to organizations – like parks, school grounds and campuses. Others, like the streets on which the neighborhood group gets together to bike, are not. Some places are indoors. Some are outdoors. Almost ANY place can be used to host Simple Community. Try to consider as many options as possible. Though I used softball as an example, sports and parks are only one kind of place where Simple Community can grow. Many shopping malls have walking programs in the hours before the stores open. Community green gardens serve several purposes. Not only do they provide fresh produce, but they also become a place of gathering, discussion and shared learning. And of course, schools, houses of worship, and the buildings owned by businesses and organizations have all kinds of places that can be used for Simple Community during non-operating hours.

In order to use places, the intended purpose of the space relative to the

opportunity for using it for Simple Community has to be taken into account. For example, a softball field is always intended for playing softball, but we can't make the assumption that we have the same permission or priority to use a field located at a high school that we might have at a local park or on a college campus.

For both high school and college the primary use of the field is to support education. The field is there for teaching, not Simple Community. One school may have strict policies about using its facilities based on its philosophy of teaching. Focus and concentration on learning may be so important that they have decided not to allow any outside influences or distractions. Another school may have the opposite philosophy, believing that an essential part of learning is to involve people from the community in virtually everything they do.

An illustration: Houses of worship as a place to build community.

There are thousands of houses of worship in America. Many of these are magnificent facilities with classrooms, playgrounds, even gymnasiums. Others have significant green space where some have built formal sports fields. When I was in junior and senior high school, I was most fortunate to have a group of about 30 friends. Many times in the summer, we would get together in the early evenings to play softball at a church softball field. I don't know that any of us were members or actually attended services at that church, but those softball games are among the very best memories of my youth.

I am thankful that the church allowed us to use the field. We never asked, they never kicked us off. As near as I can tell, we were the only ones who used the field fully or with any regularity for any purpose. I think about how many religious facilities are fully used one day per week and sit vacant for the other six. What an incredible place for building Simple Community. The beauty of our softball games is that they happened without a purpose or agenda on the part of the church. Here I am, 40 years later, still remembering the games fondly and thinking positively of the church. I could say similar things about all the basketball games I have played in church gyms over the years.

If you have a larger vision for building Simple Community you may be tempted to start by building the place, but larger places already exist. In most cases they were neither designed for nor intended to cultivate Simple Community. For example, high schools and colleges are designed with education in mind. Houses of worship are for religion. Simple Community can happen in these places too, just not as the highest priority.

Other places, like parks, are intended to be used for community. Roughly

one third of adults go to a park every week. That translates into a lot of Simple Community and even greater opportunity. What the parks need are more people, resources, traditions, and stories to make the most of Simple Community. At this point, very few places suitable for building Simple Community at the big-picture level are being fully utilized and activities in those places are not nearly as rich as they could be if all the ingredients were present.

Sports in context

You have probably noticed that many of the illustrations of Simple Community involve or are centered on sports. Without a doubt there are more sporting events and sports venues suited for cultivating Simple Community than all other contexts combined. Sports provide both participation and spectator activity. They are great as a starting point, but the opportunities extend much further. The more we learn about – and work with – places, the more I hope passionate people will build activities around everything from gardening to debate, from walking to music, from sewing to wood work and so on.

Places combined with resources:

It turns out that places are also key to my dream of seeing $30 billion dollars per year invested in Simple Community.

Before electronic communication, nearly all business was community-based and done face-to-face. Storeowners were not worried about losing touch with the needs of their customers because they interacted with them constantly. Electronic communication and the Internet changed that.

The personal connection to customers wasn't lost solely because of electronic communication, however. America used to have thousands of neighborhood hardware stores, drug stores, markets, dairies, lumber yards, banks, and so on. Each was a separate business owned and run by someone living in the neighborhood. The ability to consolidate services has made it possible for one company to own hundreds and sometimes thousands of little stores today.

Now, Americans are very rarely engaged in purchasing the necessities of life directly from their neighbors. The key word here is "directly." Millions of people work behind the scenes to support the Wal-Mart, McDonald's, and BP gas stations in America. The front line workers who are cashiers and serve customers are entry-level service workers in the most transient of jobs so they don't stay in one position for long. I have a morning coffee routine and have grown fond of

the people at the coffee shop near my office. Unfortunately, about the time I get to know a name of a worker, they leave.

Your vision of big business owners may include mansions and private jets. These days, you may not enjoy that view. But the people who own or work in large companies and retail store chains are people who want more Simple Community too. Yes, even the owners. And it is not just the billionaires who are owners. If you have a retirement fund, 401k program, savings account, stocks or mutual funds, you probably own a piece of a major company. So YOU are also an owner. Progress is good, but a byproduct is that we no longer see, face-to-face, how our purchases of goods and services continue to provide paychecks for our neighbors. Although it turns out we do still support each other in our buying and with our work, it is no longer personal or community-centered.

Just like you, owners and workers miss the close interactions between neighbors. For years companies have tried to find a way to return to a more personal way of doing business profitably. Unfortunately, the advantages that make building large retail stores profitable are a financial deterrent to being personally involved with the customers.

For example, people who own private hamburger stands have to take the time to buy tomatoes themselves and pay full price for them because they don't get the bulk discount. A hamburger chain like McDonald's, on the other hand, can buy millions of tomatoes at once to distribute to its restaurants. The company benefits both because of the discount price they get for buying so much and because they don't have to pay a staff member at each restaurant to buy tomatoes everyday.

At the same time, big companies have seen the personal connection with customers disappearing. Many want to do meaningful things at the neighborhood and small town level – to reconnect – but aren't able to because they no longer have the relationships or community connections. As a result, companies have been mostly left with choosing between doing nothing and doing very big things – like sponsoring major sports. Sponsorships may be noticed all over the country, but they don't have a local, more personal connection or impact.

To give you a sense of the difference between the big and the small, compare National Football League games to high school football games. Although almost all Americans have heard of the NFL, it is not an effective vehicle for establishing personal connections because there are only 32 teams and eight home games per season. Add to that, over 50,000 people attend a game - too many to provide any

kind of personal experience.

On the other hand, a high school football game is really quite intimate. There may be only hundreds or a few thousand people at the game, but the people know each other, they usually have a personal connection to the school AND there are over 25,000 high schools in America. It is real – and simple – community. Here is the catch. The relative simplicity of working with the NFL – contacting one league that controls 32 teams – is not yet found at the neighborhood level. The primary goal of the Building Simple Community side of the book is to provide an initial unified way for high schools, colleges, parks and other places to develop and run community activities in ways that companies can support them to provide real value for neighborhoods.

Both companies and communities would benefit from a unified approach to working together. Large companies get thousands of requests per week to support programs and activities. For a company to realistically be able to support community activities, it would have to have the same advantages McDonald's has buying tomatoes. It would have to organize a program to oversee services to many small communities.

Supporting fifteen different community parades is a large enough task to require considerable effort and cost, but too small to have real value to a sponsoring company. Many companies, however, would consider one BIG parade, or 1,000 small parades. In the case of one big parade, it would work because it would be publicized to a national TV audience. The parade would no doubt be near the company's headquarters, largest store or factory. The Macy's Parade in New York is an obvious example.

If a company could support 1,000 parades, they would be able to touch most of their employees, partners and customers directly. That kind of impact makes good business sense, but it just wouldn't be cost effective for those companies to start from scratch to build or support 1,000 independent parades. On the other hand, if companies could simply, efficiently and successfully enhance an organization that coordinates 1,000 parades that already exist, it would make great business sense for them to make investments in events like parades.

National organizations – like colleges, high schools and parks – have locations throughout the country that are conducive to Simple Community and provide the scale needed to draw serious resources from companies. The building of Simple Community works by bringing organizations with thousands of places together with companies that have the desire and resources to make wonderful

events happen.

Some of you are probably wondering how supporting 1,000 groups can be any more personal than sponsoring the NFL or the Macy's Parade. The key is this: All thousand groups will agree to do a few, key things in the same way. They can do everything else in whatever way they want.

The following is a hypothetical example. Ford decides to sponsor high school homecoming parades. They will provide the cash to buy chicken wire and paper for any float, as long as a Ford truck pulls it and the parade starts, ends, or goes by the Ford dealer. Now was that painful? I bet you were thinking it was going to be some unrelated marketing attack. If building Simple Community is going to work, and it can and should, people will want the productive company connections, which will be neither assaulting nor insulting. The goal of companies providing resources for Simple Community is to have people say, "Oh, good, you are here. Thank you for doing this."

Again, you may well be thinking that it is impossible for a company to market in a way that will make you feel grateful for its involvement. However, I would like to convince you otherwise. Here are the basics, please read Building Simple Community to get the full picture.

Start by thinking about how a company's product or service makes your life better by providing something you need or desire. Then think about key moments and events in life that can be linked to that need or desire. Work to link the events directly with the company's product or service in an unexpected, but welcomed, way. When it is possible to find a connection, it is remarkable. And that is precisely the goal, to be REMARK-able. It is possible for a company to achieve remarkableness by following five steps:

Start by thinking of a life-changing event: riding a bike. Once you learn, you are a bike-rider for the rest of your life.

Realize that the best remarkable experiences are unforgettable: most of us remember the first time we rode a bike. Even more parents remember the first time one of their children rode a bike.

Evaluate what the company can do related to this experience to make the moment even better: a bike company committed to teaching parents how to teach their kids – and reminding you to capture it on film! Do YOU have pictures of the first time? I definitely remember it, but I don't have pictures. A bike company has an opportunity here.

Seek out the special kinds of experiences that will become stories to tell time

and time again: the story about your child's first bike ride will never get old. The company benefits because you will mention them on some of the occasions that you show the picture or video. Also, every time you think of buying a bike, you will remember the company.

Finally, know that the best of the best remarkable experiences are those that come from the heart. This is where the personal connection comes back to the company. Even though no person from the company was there when the remarkable experience happened, enough people will mention the company with appreciation when they tell their stories that both sides benefit.

Not all remarkable experiences build Simple Community. Many, like the above, make the lives of individuals and families better. There are more examples when you flip the book that are mostly intended to remind those who make a living by selling things that they are people who buy things too. There are also new ideas about marketing. The more we do to personalize our thinking about how and when products and services are used, the more REAL good we can provide – rather than just messages – and the more we can provide resources for a richer Simple Community life.

Stories and Traditions

When you go out for the evening to a social event and the next day a friend asks how it went, you will usually respond in one of two ways. If it was nothing special, you will answer in five words or less: "Fine" or, perhaps, "It was ok." Maybe it won't even warrant a word, just a dismissive grunt. If you had a great time, though, you will tell a story. It is really the only way to do it, "It was so funny, right when I got there..," or, "You wouldn't believe it, but..." Stories are the proof that Simple Community took place.

Traditions are even better. When you find a context for social gathering that you really love, chances are that the group of people you share it with will find a reason to encourage the same thing to happen again and again. While you may perhaps find that an odd definition of tradition, think of the traditions in your own life and read on.

By the time you are done with this chapter you will easily be able to tell when the best of Simple Community is happening. If you are lucky, you may even be able to encourage it to happen more often because of what you know about stories and traditions.

Stories:

Think of the stories you tell in your life and how often you tell stories. One of the things I love most about my wife Vicki is her story telling. I love going out with her or having friends over, because I know – regardless of the setting – she will have a great story to tell and everyone will love it. Great story telling involves one part how you tell it and ten parts living a life rich in experiences that produce great stories. Vicki has a wonderfully rich life, full of interests and involvement. As if that's not enough, she is always starting something new. Her life, then, is a constant source of stories.

As with people and traditions, stories can't be forced. If you are living a rich life, the stories will come. You don't build a rich life or Simple Community with stories. Rather, you can get a great sense of the progress you are making by listening for stories. If don't hear any, something is missing. If there are stories, they will tell you what is at the heart of the success and give you clues about how

to invest your resources to increase the richness of your life.

Stories also help in welcoming others to your Simple Community experience. The story illustrates what is at the heart of your Simple Community, not the process or the ingredients. When you buy a car, you don't go to a show room and see a bunch of parts on the floor. You see the whole car. They don't show you how it is put together. They let you drive it. You don't buy it for the parts and he processes, but for the car and the experience.

Traditions:

I want to offer a novel approach for defining tradition. I am not as interested in its literal meaning as I am in what it provides and what it has to do with our need and desire for Simple Community. Tradition provides the best security in social settings. The more secure we feel in social settings, the more we engage and feel free to be ourselves. I have said "I am just not up for it," many times when an opportunity to go to a party or other social gathering was presented to me. Tradition, however, makes it nearly impossible to decline. If I can get out of it, the event's status as a tradition is in question.

Let me break down a tradition with this true story. Many years ago, three friends and I went to Myrtle Beach for a weekend of golf. This was early enough in our careers that the cost represented quite an investment. To make it work, we rented one hotel room with two double beds. The room rate was about $15 a night (it's about $60 now). Duane is not a small man, so the first thing we did when we got to the hotel was flip a coin to see who got stuck sleeping with Duane. Then we ate breakfast at a really bad ham-n-egger. Then we played golf. Then had dinner, where we talked about meaning-of-life stuff. We played putt-putt afterwards and finished with Dairy Queen. In one of the first years, the discussion at Dairy Queen got so heated that one of us walked the mile back to the hotel.

That is the setup. That was more than 25 years ago. A tradition was born. We have been back every year. We stay at the same hotel or a similar one – but now we stay in two rooms instead of one (we still flip to see who gets stuck with Duane). We still play putt-putt, eat dinner together, and go to Dairy Queen. The tradition of Dairy Queen, to see who takes the walk, still lives.

The first time we went, we knew that we were on to something special. It had nothing to do with the list of things that we repeat in nearly the exact same way every year. It certainly had nothing to do with the quality of golf. What evolved was the realization that once a year we were completely candid with each other

and talked about what the previous year contributed to our lives. We have been more open and gone to deeper parts of life in those weekends than at any other time. We long and yearn for that opportunity.

Tradition didn't make our golf weekend happen. The awareness of an opportunity for deep community called us to unconsciously establish traditions that would encourage – no – demand that we do it again and in the same way.

I think we repeat traditions for two reasons. First, after we've captured lightning in a bottle once, we want to do it again. A tradition is born on the heels of a magical event. When a splendidly wonderful moment of Simple Community happens, everyone involved wants it to be repeated. So we try to imitate it and get as close to the initial experience as possible. Along with that commitment is the dedication to be as involved the second time as we were the first.

The second reason that we repeat traditions is to create a safety blanket. In a tradition, things are repeated – even dumb unintended things like the walk from Dairy Queen. The stronger the tradition is, the more precise the formula. This prescription of activities removes the need to wonder or worry about what might happen in the particular social setting.

I don't know anyone who likes to be uncomfortable in social settings. With a tradition, you know what to do. You know the others. You know what they will do. The potential for social mishaps becomes miniscule because many of the aspects of the event are comfortably programmed into the tradition. In repeating the tradition, the focus is to have another opportunity to experience the wonderful event that caused the lightning in a bottle in the first place.

Every time you repeat a tradition, it either becomes stronger and more routine or it moves closer to its end. The repetition in strong traditions is at the heart of many substantial moments and events. Political groups, religions, social clubs, and family gatherings are all steeped in traditions, which foster our ability to enjoy the most meaningful components of life.

Among my greatest gifts in life are the long-standing traditions I have with people who I love dearly. Tradition is speaking to us from a voice deep within. It is telling us just how vast our need is for richer community. So many traditions have been lost or moved to the background through a combination of different changes, but our need is still there.

There may be a temptation to create traditions, but create Simple Community instead. Just like stories, traditions must happen of their own accord. Look for places and opportunities where you can develop Simple Community ideas. Then

watch as life unfolds. Listen for stories. Be patient.

A normal experience like eating dinner can turn into Thanksgiving. The significance or fulfillment that came in one special moment is the seed. When two or more people realize that they have just experienced something special, you have the opportunity for tradition. Repeat it.

Before you do it again, ask yourself what it was about the experience that made it unique. It is often something quirky or even silly – like flipping a coin to see who sleeps with Duane. The second time you do the activity, reintroduce the quirky aspect. It is the marker, the commemoration of the importance of the first event. If the quirky thing sticks, if the event is still meaningful the second time, and the third, then maybe, just maybe, you are nurturing a tradition.

Tradition is a powerful supporter of Simple Community, because the people partaking in the event are there to celebrate and honor the power of the first experience. Often, that is enough. It is a foundation of security that opens the door to many more fun and meaningful opportunities. You shouldn't need to force the significance of the experience. If the first time resonated with people, they will want to be involved again.

As a bond among those who share in them, traditions go a long way towards building a safe environment for deep fulfillment in Simple Community. Although their very nature and quirkiness can scare outsiders away, they can also be tempting, and an experience that others want to be a part of. If your community has a tradition that can be extended, welcome new people and introduce them to your event's history and charm.

The final great power of tradition is its ability to capture us. If you are part of a tradition, you know what I mean. Tradition creates priority. When you are too busy to invest in Simple Community, your traditions will sustain you.

By the way, it's never too late to start. Duane was in his 40s the first time we went to Myrtle Beach and he just retired from the group at age 70. He never got any better at golf.

A Call to Action

I would like to leave you with ideas for quick, easy starters for building Simple Community in case you decide not to flip the book and keep reading. They are in no particular order and serve as a very rough summary of the calls to action from within the book.

Remember, that when asked what they need the most, most Americans say time with family and friends. This means that more people probably want to do something with you than you think. Don't be shy. Ask. Maybe you think someone is too busy, but what is the worst thing that can happen? Even if they say no, at least you did something to try and connect, not just for you, but for them too – being asked probably made them feel better.

Remember that time with family and friends is much more about being with them than about what you do with them. SO KEEP IT SHORT, CLOSE AND SIMPLE. The odds are you will do much more.

Time is your only treasure. You probably have more than you think. It might help a lot to monitor how you spend your time for a while to see what you truly treasure. You will be surprised. You also get to decide if you like what you see or if you want to choose to do something else with your life.

What is your story? Better, what is your newest story? How often is your life producing a new story? I really believe life provides new stories every day. We just need to start being more aware of them. Sometimes Simple Community starts by talking to ourselves! I often go to sleep by asking myself what new stories the day had for me. I am often surprised at what simple and wonderful things come to mind. I am also often thankful. The alternative is going to bed worrying about the economy, the wars or something else. Both the stories and the economy will be there in the morning. A better night's sleep started with a story of life brings hope in the morning.

What are your traditions? You have them. You really do. Maybe you don't call

them that, but you have things you do the same way at certain intervals. They provide comfort or you wouldn't be doing them. Personal traditions – or rituals – are great too. Maybe as you think of traditions with others you come up empty. Do you remember some you used to have? Traditions can be revived…

STOP PAYING ATTENTION! Technology is great. But it is a tool to make life better. It is not the reason for living. Every time you find yourself wondering how technology will fix something stop and ask how life will help too. Then go for a walk.

Talk to someone – anyone – about Simple Community. Pick a person you think might have a passion to build it too. Ask them if they think we need more Simple Community too and just let it go from there.

Think about the people you know. Who would benefit most from reading this book? The benefit can go one of two ways:

One, this is someone who personally needs more Simple Community. If that is the case, go for a walk with them and give them the book.

Two, this is someone who is in a position to do a whole lot to extend the contexts or resources for building Simple Community. Same thing. Walk, talk, flip the book over, and give to them.

Now give your book away and go play!

(Endnotes)

1 A trend that grew from four million square feet of new construction a year in 2004 to 14 million in 2008: according to *Property & Profile* research – reported in the *Wall Street Journal* July 17, 2008 B1.

2 Reported in *Fast Company* July, 2000

3 Attendance statistics from *Minor League Baseball* through 2008

4 *Deseret News* (Salt Lake City) March 27, 2005 – by the way, it's free! The folks at *Field of Dreams* believe in Simple Community too.

5 Peterson, MJ. (1995) *"The Emergence of a Mass Market for Fax Machines." Technology & Society,* 17 (4) 469-82.

6 I found the study years ago. It was conducted by UCSD Professor Herbert I. Schiller and his students. It was a small and not conclusive study and I don't go into greater detail here because the results are not important. The bigger point is this: if a recent study of information use relative to information availability is possible, if you know of it, please let me know!

7 *PR Newswire*, May 2, 2007

8 What?!? Not baseball??? Almost certainly not. Though sports like baseball and college football from time to time drew audiences of over 10,000 (foreshadowing their future dominance) far fewer people lived in larger cities and more than half worked in farming jobs. Football and baseball got a lot of press, but most Americans weren't directly exposed. You can think of them as being in the *"Anticipation Phase"* during the 1800s. See: T*he Rise and Fall of American Sport* by Ted Vincent: (Bison Books 1981) to get a feel for emerging sports during the 1880s.

9 *The Dumbest Generation: How the Digital Age Stupefies Young Americans and Jeopardizes Our Future.* Mark Bauerlein (2008). Tarcher-Penguin.

10 I'm pretty sure my dissertation is available through the *University of Michigan* by searching Richard Luker and 1986.

11 As an example, the following statistics came from the front page of *USA Today*, July 16, 2008.

12 This came from analysis of U.S. government Labor statistics and research from the Conference Board.

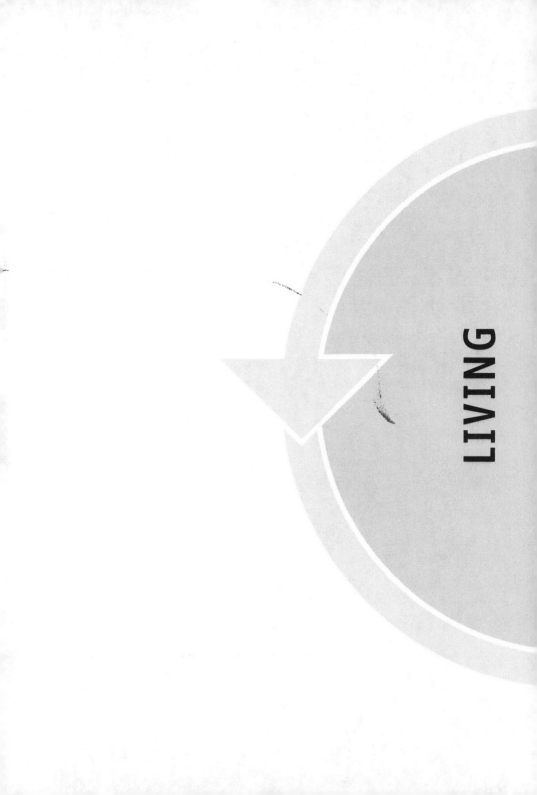

LIVING

BUILDING